HOW TO TALK YOUR WAY TO SUCCESS

Also by Paul J. Micali:
The Lacy Techniques of Salesmanship

HOW TO TALK YOUR WAY TO SUCCESS

The secrets of effective business communication

Paul J. Micali

President, The Lacy Institute

E. P. Dutton, Inc.   New York

The excerpts on pages 86 through 88 are from "Voice Coaches Claim the Election Campaign Could Use More Tone," by Nicholas Gage, in the *Wall Street Journal*, April 23, 1968. Reprinted with the permission of the *Wall Street Journal*, © 1968 by Dow Jones & Company, Inc.

Published in the United States by E.P. Dutton, Inc., 2 Park Avenue, New York, N.Y. 10016

Library of Congress Cataloging in Publication Data

Micali, Paul J.
    How to talk your way to success.

    1. Public speaking. I. Title
PN4121.M553   1983   808.5′1   83–9003

ISBN: 0-525-48086-2

Published simultaneously in Canada by
Fitzhenry & Whiteside Limited, Toronto
W
10 9 8 7 6 5 4 3 2 1

Revised Edition

To Jim, Mo, and Donna

A copybook found in an Egyptian tomb over three thousand years ago contained this maxim: "Make yourself a craftsman in speech for thereby you shall gain the upper hand."

Contents

Preface

In spite of the many new and sophisticated methods of communication now available in the modern world, the spoken word still remains of critical importance. This situation is not apt to change, *ever*. People will always speak to each other, often on impulse. And because so little attention is given to the subject "How to speak well" in our early, formative years, bad speaking habits are picked up and kept for a lifetime. What's even worse is that most individuals don't recognize these habits within themselves and go through life wondering why they are ineffective.

The telephone, television, meetings, conventions, assemblies, seminars, church services, school and college classes all depend on verbal communication. Every single day of our lives is influenced by what we say or by what someone said to us or by how it was said. Think of the last time you were feeling low and you needed someone to give you a compliment or praise of some sort and, luckily, it happened. For hours afterwards, and perhaps until you fell asleep that night, you savored those kind words. Now think about the last time that someone attacked you verbally. Your boss, your spouse, or a friend unmercifully raked you over the coals. Those harsh words stayed in your mind for *days*. They were damaging to you. But you remembered more than just the *words* fired at you. The shouting, the inflection, and the emphasis remained painfully vivid. That's just one example of the power of speech. There's an old saying: "Sticks and stones may break my bones but words will never hurt me." Forget it. It isn't true. Most broken bones will heal in six to eight weeks. Feelings, egos, and hearts that have been broken by words will take months, years, sometimes even lifetimes to heal—if they heal at all.

Regardless of your field of endeavor, success in life often will depend on how well you put yourself across when you speak. Even when you are trying to convince someone of something—when the use of logic is so important—it will usually boil down to how you came across rather than how convincing your argument was. Any trial lawyer will tell you that *how* you plead your case is vital. The evidence is certainly important; but, how it is presented (with confidence and punch, or weak and disorganized) may well determine the verdict. Here's an even more common occurrence. Suppose your boss automatically gives you a raise once a year. The year is now up and there's no raise in the paycheck. As each week goes by without the expected raise, you get progressively more angry. Finally you decide that you're going to have it out and you charge straight to the office. See what's happening? You're ready for a fight—and you know the rest. The boss resents your threatening approach, you lose brownie points in the process, and down the drain goes the raise and maybe the job as well. Had you come across as someone who wanted to know in what areas to improve in order to qualify for a raise, things would have been substantially different. *How* you ask is so vitally important.

So fundamental, you say. Everybody knows these things. It's plain common sense. Of course it is; but common sense is not so common. So few people realize the importance of speaking impressively that of the thousands of politicians in the United States there are only a handful who spend any time attempting to improve upon their speaking abilities.

Well, you're different. You are about to read a book on this important subject. It's the first step toward more powerful and effective communication. When you begin to put into practice the simple lessons presented here, you'll soon find yourself actually enjoying situations that used to make you tense and exhausted. Business meetings, presentations, and phone calls to potential clients will seem challenging opportunities that allow you to practice and polish your new skills. In time, you may even volunteer for speaking engagements before large groups. The ease and confidence you develop as you progress will be of value to you in every area of your life. And you'll reap the benefits for years to come.

1
We Are
What We Say

Remember the time you walked into that conference room, for that most important meeting—and you were "loaded for bear"? You were thoroughly armed with the facts to back up your ideas. You were oozing with confidence. You just couldn't wait for your turn to speak. Yet when your turn did come, something happened. The right words just didn't seem to flow. The facts didn't come out in the right, logical order. It was all so choppy. You knew that you weren't convincing the others. Why did this happen? Was it nervousness? Lack of practice? Inability to make an impact? A combination of all three?

Remember the day that you made a sales pitch to the buying committee of the supermarket chain? You had polished and refined your presentation so that nothing could go wrong. You had charts, graphs, sophisticated advertising research reports. You used Madison Avenue language to impress. But it didn't work. They didn't buy. When they told you their reasons for not buying, you realized that they had missed your points. Had you gotten too complicated? Had you lost your audience *because* of your elaborate efforts?

Remember that evening at the club meeting, when you were so opposed to the change in bylaws? You kept raising your hand because you wanted so much to present your sound reasons. Finally you were recognized by the president, someone stuck a microphone in front of your mouth, and the "er's" and the "ah's" that came out were so embarrassing. You stammered and sputtered, something you never do. And you left out the most important reason. You didn't realize that until afterward, when it was too late. What happened? Was something foreign to you? The audience? The excitement? The microphone? All three?

There have been situations, I'm sure, that you have experienced that paralleled, if not completely coincided with, the ones just mentioned. In each case you most likely wished that you could have been more effective in your efforts to communicate verbally. Well, becoming more effective requires an understanding of the five common mistakes that people regularly make—and knowing how to avoid them.

What are these mistakes?

1. Making a bad first impression.
2. Not speaking clearly, being plagued by bad speech habits.
3. Speaking over people's heads.
4. Becoming a victim of nervous tension.
5. Failing to make an impact.

Let's start with the first one.

We are all judged by others—quickly, by first impressions. This judging process is often complex; many factors can be involved, such as the house we live in, the neighborhood in which it's located, the car we drive, the clothes we wear, the clubs to which we belong, the schools we attended, and so forth. But most of these things seem to take a back seat to the first impression we create once we begin to speak. What comes out of our mouths is absorbed and evaluated, almost instantly, and the listener swiftly arrives at a first impression. If it's the right type, we're okay for now but subject to further evaluation. If it's the wrong type we've had it. Bad impressions stick—rather permanently.

Take the daily experiences of the unknown stand-up comic who plays theaters, nightclubs, fairs —anywhere, to be discovered. His livelihood depends on making a good first impression—consistently. He is given a big introduction by the master of ceremonies who tells the audience how lucky they are to be catching the act of a "big time" comedian. Naturally, since they've never heard of this comic, they don't believe a word the MC says. Finally, the comedian nervously comes on, in the midst of the light applause that's been asked for, and the first-impression test is upon him. If the first joke he tells is extremely funny and gets them rolling in the aisles, the rest of his performance is golden. He gains more momentum each time he opens his mouth. When he's through he gets a tremendous, unsolicited ovation and people want to know his name. But let that first joke lay an egg, and he's had it from that audience. They immediately decide that he's small-time stuff and from then on, no matter how comical or creative he becomes, getting a laugh is almost impossible. And all through this painful experience he keeps telling himself, "I've gotta get a better opener."

Some years ago, as New England sales manager for a pharmaceutical manufacturer, I was in the process of recruiting a sales representative for the Worcester, Massachusetts, area. At that time the company had a strict policy: To be hired as a sales representative, an applicant had to be either a registered pharmacist or possess a premedical degree. No one else could be considered. So, when screening the resumés, it was customary to eliminate first those who did not show the proper qualifications. One applicant had sent me a most interesting resumé. It was cleverly written and it was obvious that he was aggressive—a sought-after quality in salespeople in any industry. Yet his schooling in no way met our requirements for consideration. Neither did his sales experience. He had been successful at selling floor tile in a retail store and felt that he was capable of bigger and better things.

The day after I had placed his resumé in the "do-not-qualify" file, I received a phone call from Harry Grover. He was polite but firm. There was a warmth in his voice. He opened by admitting that he knew that he did not qualify for the position, but all he was asking for was a fifteen-minute interview. I explained delicately that it would be a waste of time for both of us, but he could not accept that. I finally agreed, against my better judgment, to grant him an interview. I was going to spend an entire day in Worcester interviewing applicants so I scheduled him to be my last interview, at 4:30 P.M. I looked at it as a public relations effort for my company. I would be nice to him but I would polish him off in fifteen minutes and be on my way back to the Boston area, ahead of the traffic.

At 4:27 P.M. the phone rang in my room at the Bancroft Hotel. It was Harry calling from the lobby. I told him to "come on up." At 4:30 sharp he was knocking at my door. I opened it and there stood a little guy—about five feet, two inches tall with a big smile. As we shook hands, he said, with a pleasant smile, "I'm here to dedicate myself to the growth of our company." ("*Our* company," I said to myself; he sure assumes a lot in a hurry.) But before he started his second, well-planned sentence, I noticed something else about him that floored me. He had *my* catalog of products under *his* left arm.

Of the over five hundred people I had interviewed over the years, not one had taken the trouble, in advance, to become familiar with our products. Yet Harry not only walked in with our catalog, but he proceeded to tell me all about my company, its origin, its sales record—and then asked me to quiz him on the products. I did and he was unbelievable. He had practically memorized that catalog. Through it all he spoke in a warm, convincing fashion. There was excitement in his voice. He showed no nervousness through his speech or facial expressions. His gestures were natural yet significant. He put himself across superbly. As I marveled at this theoretically unqualified creature, his first statement kept coming back to me: "I'm here to dedicate myself to the growth of *our* company."

I hired Harry because I believed in him. My first impression of him dictated my action. There was much flak from the home office. Technically he didn't qualify for the job, they claimed, and his chances of succeeding were slim. I will admit that he had a rocky start, but within a year he was among the top salespeople in the country. He thanked me profusely, many times, for giving him the opportunity and having faith in him. But each time I told him that he did it by himself.

THINK BEFORE YOU SPEAK

Harry had given much thought to just how he would go about making a good first impression. Most people don't take the time or the trouble to even think about it. Then they wonder why they come across poorly when they speak. The predicament is self-styled. Regularly they give little (if any) advance thought to what they're about to say. And since their thoughts are not organized, what comes out is merely a flow of words that are hard to follow. Even worse, they are apt to mean nothing.

Joe Average each day comes in contact with at least a dozen people he knows. He speaks to them almost automatically. He says the usual things and gets the usual answers. Each conversation goes like this:

"Hi, Jack, how are you?"

"Fine, Joe, how are you?"

"Fine."

"How have you been, Jack?"

"Fine, Joe, how have you been?"

"Fine, and how's everything?"

"Fine, how's everything with you?"

"Fine."

What did it all mean? Were they really checking the physical well-being of each other? Did they really mean what they said to each other or was it a stereotyped flow of words denoting that neither knew what to say upon meeting? The latter is usually the case. Too often it takes several sentences of sour nothings before two people can settle down to a half-decent conversation. Why is it so? No thinking before speaking. Yet it's so easy to be different from everybody else. It really doesn't take that much thought. For instance, instead of "Hi, how are you?" imagine how different and more favorable a reaction Joe Average would get if he greeted people with "Hi, Jack, how nice to see you"; or, "What a pretty shade of green you're wearing, Mary"; or, "Hi, Jim, that's a good-looking tie." Opening statements such as these mean much more than "How are you?"; "How are you doing?"; "How's everything?" At first, making this change will seem strange. You will feel most unusual; and you will be just that. You will have raised yourself out of the rut that so many people seem to be in. And in the process more people will actually listen to what you have to say.

Unimpressive daily conversations are also brought about by the ego. We inflict upon others information about ourselves in which they have absolutely no interest. We should realize that they are only interested in themselves. Psychological tests have indicated that 94 percent of the time people are thinking about themselves. Now that's a very high percentage and to expect others to be impressed by us when we talk only about ourselves is foolish.

Here's a favorite story that makes this point quite forcefully. A mature, well-dressed Wall Street banker had car trouble on his way to work one morning in the Bronx and he ended up taking the subway. Naturally, the subway crowd showed no more respect for him than anyone else, so he got pushed and shoved in normal style. He was annoyed and most irritated. Finally, he couldn't stand being quiet about it any longer. He turned to the little guy in overalls, carrying a lunch box and hanging on to the strap next to his, and said, "You know, I hate this subway. I never ride on it. As a matter of fact this is the first time I have been compelled to ride it in over ten years." At which the little guy most emphatically replied, "Mister, you couldn't possibly have the slightest idea of just how much we've missed you."

If only we could train ourselves *always* to stop a moment (even a few seconds will do it) just before we speak and think about what we are going to say. It can be done. It's just a case of remembering to do it. We can think much faster than we can speak, so it's not an impossible undertaking under any circumstances.

The rewards are many. For one thing, you will never again have to apologize for saying the wrong thing at the wrong time. (Think of how many times you've had to say, "I didn't mean that the way it sounded.") More importantly, you can't put yourself across in the right light if you go through life giving little thought to what you are about to say.

Perhaps if you regard every opening statement as vital to a good first impression you will get into the habit of thinking before speaking.

That's step number one. There's much more.

2
Speaking So They Can Understand You— The Basics

Most Americans say that they like to listen to people with foreign accents. Did you ever stop to wonder why this is so? Most likely, it's partly because their accents are refreshingly different, but more importantly, it's generally true that when foreigners speak English they are trying so hard to be understood that they speak as distinctly as they possibly can. It may be that native Americans think they like the accent when what they really like is the slower pace and more dramatic emphasis most foreigners bring to their speech. Because we've all met people with foreign accents that were so difficult to understand it was downright painful to listen to them.

It's one thing when a nonnative speaker slurs and garbles what he has to say, but what about all those people who have grown up speaking English and who have developed such poor speech patterns that they might as well be speaking a foreign language? It seems that every day of our lives we find ourselves saying to someone, "I'm sorry, would you please repeat what you said?" Does this suggest that we are all somewhat hard of hearing? Hardly. What it does indicate is that most people do not speak so that they can be clearly understood. Some speak too rapidly and certain words are just lost in the shuffle. Others may simply turn away from you and speak in another direction, making it almost impossible for you to hear them. Then there are others who don't compensate for noises around them by speaking louder in order that others can hear them. But the vast majority who must regularly be asked to repeat what they have just said are the ones who just simply don't open their mouths when speaking. They practically keep their teeth clenched together, making it extremely difficult for people to understand what is being said. Research has shown that Americans, in general, are careless and sloppy talkers. We'll learn how to correct the usual causes later on.

TO BE HEARD IS FUNDAMENTAL

When you speak to people you are doing a very significant thing. With your words you sell your ideas by appealing to the listeners' reason, and with your voice you are reaching them through their instinct or subconscious mind. If the voice is not loud enough or clear enough for listeners to understand what you are saying, all aspects of communication have been lost. Yet, in failing to project, most people reduce their tonal volume to such a degree that it requires the listener to possess an extremely keen sense of hearing.

Two things are wrong here. First of all, we must assume that most people have a normal sense of hearing. It is rare when you find someone whose hearing is much above normal. Secondly, when not speaking loudly enough, we are actually expecting listeners to concentrate much more than they usually do and, in the process, they are straining their hearing abilities in order to catch every pearl of wisdom. The average individual is not willing to do this. Based on the theory that we are all as lazy as we dare to be, this would be expecting a great deal and it is rarely received.

Furthermore, we must realize that an older person's hearing is apt to have deteriorated due to the aging process. (And many people who are hard of hearing even in this day and age refuse to resort to the very sophisticated hearing aids that are available.) So, when you take all of these factors into consideration, you will have to agree that it makes a great deal of sense to project with our speaking voice on a constant basis.

Not too long ago a salesman who had taken one of our sales courses was having trouble closing a very large sale with a potential new account. He regularly sat down with the sales manager to develop strategy. Then he would go back to make his presentation to the same buyer, only to end up with a "we'll-think-it-over" answer. He knew that if he made this particular sale it would practically double his territorial volume—that's how important it was to him. Yet it just seemed impossible to get his foot in the door. His sales manager finally called me and asked if I would consider making a call on this account with the salesman involved. He felt that maybe I could help him close the sale, and if not, make a determination as to whether or not this account could be sold at all. The necessary arrangements were made and we made the call together. I asked the salesman to forget how many times he had been there and to start from scratch and make a complete presentation. I felt that if I heard the whole story I could better determine whether the strategy for making the sale was correct. The salesman did a marvelous job. He used all of the techniques necessary to properly sell his service. He displayed a marvelous sales personality, used visuals, smiled at the right places, and did just about everything that you would expect him to do in a professional selling situation. I did notice one thing, however, and it involved his ability to project. In the beginning of the interview, fired with enthusiasm, he came through very clearly and with plenty of tone quality. But as the presentation progressed his volume seemed to decrease. Towards the end he was not only speaking less enthusiastically but his volume was down considerably from the time he had started. When he asked for the order he was given the usual answer: "It sounds very good and we'll think about it and let you know."

When we went back to the car we naturally reviewed the entire presentation trying to determine what went wrong. It was quite obvious that his selling attempt was professional in nature and my only comment to the salesman was that he seemed to reduce his amount of enthusiasm towards the end of the interview. He agreed but felt that by then we had gotten down to the unimportant details of the cost of the service and its many variations in connection with the monthly billing that would be involved.

The next day I called the buyer myself. I explained to him the real reason why I had been making the call with the salesman the day before and asked for his help in determining the reason why this particular salesman, who seemed to be very successful with other aspects of his work, could not seem to succeed in selling him. The elderly, good-natured buyer was delighted to hear from me. We chatted about the young salespeople of today and how most of them are not as equipped to do the job as well as they might be. After a very warm and lengthy conversation he finally came to the point. He said, "You know, I like that boy and I really would like to give him our business. As a matter of fact, I am not completely satisfied with the company that's handling our accounts receivable now. To make a switch would be a refreshing change, provided that the cost were more reasonable and the service better than what we are getting. And speaking of cost," said the buyer, "it seems that every time this young fellow comes in and tells me what a good job he can do for me, when we get down to just how much it's going to cost, he begins to mumble. I don't understand everything he's saying. I'm embarrassed to admit that I don't wear a hearing aid and that's why I keep telling him that I'll think about it. Really, I'd love to know what his price structure is."

I called the salesman and explained the situation to him. I suggested that he write him an immediate letter, stating that he was following up on his call and attaching a complete schedule of the services he could render and the costs that such services entailed. By *return mail* he received a letter stating that the buyer was ready to give him his business and would he please come in and make the necessary arrangements.

CLARITY IS NOT HARD TO ACHIEVE

Once we have learned to open our mouths regularly when speaking, the next thing to consider is clarity. Speaking clearly is not at all difficult. It is simply a case of being completely aware of how one is coming across with each single word being uttered.

Let us suppose that you received a typewritten letter. And let us further suppose that the letter had no capital letters, no periods at the end of sentences, no paragraphs. It was simply a case of receiving several hundred words that were all run together. Imagine how hard it would be to read this letter and properly digest the contents. Now that's how many people talk. They simply go on and on and on, often in a monotone, without ever breaking off a sentence to separate it from the next. We must become completely aware that sentences end with a period and that there is a space between the end of one sentence and the beginning of the next, exactly as with the typewritten letter.

Running words together is an even greater problem. Clarity is sacrificed to a tremendous degree when this is done. As an example: it is very common for some people to say "didja" for "did you," "whenya" for "when you," "seeya" for "see you," "forum" for "for him," "tella" for "tell her," and so on. Fortunately most of the time, depending on how well we know the person who is speaking, we are able to understand what is being said. However, when listening to someone we have just met and not knowing their method of speaking, words that have been run together can prove to be a disastrous impediment to good communication.

Running together words that are poorly enunciated forces listeners to be alert in order to figure out what you are trying to tell them. They must catch every key word and then go back and decipher the sentence in their minds. While they continue to flash back mentally to figure out the previous sentences that you have uttered, they obviously miss part of the next sentence. If the portion they miss contains the key word, then they lose the entire thought. By enunciating poorly you are actually expecting mental gymnastics from your listeners. You are expecting a sustained effort on their part to decipher what you are saying and figure out what it all means.

Let's talk about sustained effort. Did you ever stop to consider how difficult it is to maintain a sustained effort in doing anything? Let's conduct a little experiment and it will drive the point home very clearly for you. Hold out your left arm at shoulder height, with index finger pointing straight ahead. (Let's do this, not just read about it.) You are pointing straight ahead with your left arm extended and you're going to hold it there for two minutes. Time yourself with your watch. Be sure to keep your arm completely extended. At the end of this time period you will find that your arm will have become extremely heavy and maybe even somewhat painful. In fact, during the second minute it will actually become an effort to hold it in that position. Now, when you consider that your arm is one of the most powerful parts of your body and yet it does not stand up that well under the sustained effort of only two minutes, imagine the mental effort you impose on your listeners, who must struggle for much longer periods in an attempt to interpret the sounds you are making. Is it any wonder that they may lose interest in what you are saying?

GOOD ENUNCIATION

Careless enunciation can easily rob you of your effectiveness when putting yourself across verbally. This habit may be having a severe negative influence on you, and yet you may be totally unaware of its existence. People never tell you that you speak indistinctly. They simply turn you off.

To improve your enunciation is not difficult and, by the way, has nothing to do with the speed with which you talk. It is impossible to talk faster than people can understand—*if you enunciate clearly*. You probably have marveled at the rapidity with which sports announcers can relate what is happening and yet be so well understood. A blow by blow description of a prizefight is a perfect example. Each punch is described as quickly as it's thrown—and many times they come fast and furiously. The secret is simply *good enunciation*. Sports commentators are not only aware of its importance but they work at it. They listen to tapes of themselves to make sure that every word is easily understood regardless of the rapid-fire delivery.

To enunciate clearly and sharply one must first understand how the act of speaking is physically accomplished. Air that comes up from your lungs strikes your vocal cords and this produces sound. Then, using chiefly your tongue, lips, and jaws, you convert that sound into words. The process of that conversion determines how much clarity there is in your enunciation. For instance, the sounds of *p* as in Paul and *b* as in boy are formed with the lips. If you utter them with relaxed instead of tense lips, you will become easier to understand. You can quickly demonstrate this fact to yourself right now. Say aloud, "Brendon Bracken brought Beaver Brook's brother, Benjamin." It is virtually impossible to say this phrase without your lips being completely relaxed.

How do you relax your lips? The quickest way to do so is to imitate the sound of a motorboat by blowing air between your lips and allowing them to flop up and down loosely. Do this several times. Now, take a deep breath and release air through your lips without necessarily making a sound but letting your lips flow vigorously up and down. Now say the following statement three times without stopping, "Brendon Bracken brought Beaver Brook's brother, Benjamin." If the second and third time you sounded better than the first, it is plainly because you relaxed your lips and in the process the sound of *b* was easier for you to make. It was enunciated in such a way that people could easily understand it.

The sounds of *t* and *d* are formed chiefly with the tongue. Say the following sentence aloud. "I think that I ought to tell Tom the time." Now relax the tongue. You can do this by imitating a machine gun by blowing your breath out, and as you do so let your tongue flop up and down against the roof of your mouth. At first this may be difficult to do, but after a few tries you'll find that it's rather easy. After you have done the machine gun exercise a few times, try the statement again. "I think that I ought to tell Tom the time." If you found this statement easier to pronounce clearly, it means that you have improved your enunciation by relaxing your tongue.

Now let's tackle the sounds of *g* and *j*. These sounds are formed chiefly with the jaws. First of all, say the following statement aloud. "Jimmy and Johnny were juggling jugs of juice." This is not easy to say if the jaws are not completely relaxed. Here is a simple exercise for the jaws. With the lower jaw hanging as loosely as possible, shake your head as if you were shaking water from your face and hair. As you do this let the jaw flop back and forth as loosely as you possibly can. It may even help you to relax more thoroughly by saying "Booo" as you do this. After you have done this a few times, take a deep breath and then repeat the following statement *three times:* "Jimmy and Johnny were juggling jugs of juice." As you say it you will find that it becomes easier and easier to enunciate the many j's in the sentence simply because your jaws are now completely relaxed.

I am not by any means suggesting that you have to engage in these exercises every day in order to enunciate clearly. It's simply a case of being completely aware of how to relax the lips, the tongue, and the jaws and of realizing that such relaxation affords us the ability to enunciate clearly. But if you are about to give a talk to a group and you find yourself unusually tense, doing these exercises in a private place just before you are introduced will prove extremely helpful.

Another way to ensure the use of good enunciation is to formulate mental images of the exact spelling of the words being used. For instance, a majority of Americans will say *noozpaper* instead of *newspaper*. Yet they say *few* instead of *foo*. The correct enunciation of *new* is rarely heard. Surveys have shown that the most commonly used words are the ones that are most likely to be poorly or incorrectly pronounced. For instance, many people say *Mundee, Toozdee, Frydee, dolla, paypa*, and so on. By forming a mental image of the spelling of these words, the person uttering them could realize immediately that they are being grossly mispronounced.

Strange as it may seem, people appreciate good speakers who enunciate clearly, not because of their good enunciation but because they are so refreshingly different. The problem of poor enunciation is extremely widespread. Much as we become careless over the things we do on a regular basis because they're a little boring, we also become careless in our speech habits. This carelessness almost always emerges in the form of poor enunciation.

It is important to note, however, that the practice of good enunciation can be grossly overdone. To enunciate meticulously and in an exaggerated fashion to the extent that one's speech becomes staccato is very wrong. The choppiness that is produced in so doing becomes very irritating to the listener. Furthermore, the speaker comes across as a very affected individual who is thoroughly impressed with the sound of his own voice and the manner in which he speaks. He quickly, and regularly, turns people off. The main point we are making here is that clear enunciation is imperative for verbal communication but it must not be exaggerated to the degree that it becomes too obvious and, in many cases, even annoying.

One of the best ways to improve upon your enunciation is by reading aloud whenever you possibly can. It's a marvelous exercise because it slows down the tempo of your speaking and at the same time it forces you to mouth each word exactly as you see it in print. Years ago I had the pleasure of working with a well-known newscaster on radio. Before he went on the air with the news he would, naturally, go over the yellow sheets that he had torn off the teletype machine. But he didn't just glance over the news before reading these sheets on the air. He actually went into an unused studio, closed the door, and read each news item aloud. This gave him a *feel* for the words. Not one word would be foreign to him when he went on the air. When two words in succession were rather difficult to pronounce, he would make a mark between them. A slight pause—when he came to that mark—avoided poor enunciation.

This dry run was something for which he always made time. He knew that it made for smoother delivery and it served as a constant opportunity to improve his diction. He spoke so well that people noticed it and commented on it. I repeatedly was intrigued by his ability to speak so well and yet not draw attention to his enunciation. I asked him about it one day. I said, "Dan, how do you constantly keep yourself from falling into the bad speech habits that we so regularly find in most people?" His answer was a very simple one. He said, "That's easy. I read aloud at every opportunity that I have—even at home, when I'm reading a book. If you read aloud, you hear yourself speaking and you can concentrate on how you sound as well as what you read. If you listen to yourself without watching for someone's reaction, you are able to improve upon your speaking on a regular basis."

YOU ALREADY OWN A MAGIC MIRROR

There is another type of dry run that will pay big dividends. It is the regular use of a mirror to note how we come across to others. All of us use a mirror on a daily basis. Women look into one approximately fourteen times a day, and men average four to five times a day. The only reason for this is grooming. Imagine what we could learn about how we come across to others if we were to have discussions with ourselves before a mirror. Most homes have at least one full-length mirror. By looking at all of you while you make a pitch to yourself you will learn much about what you must do to appear, act, and talk more convincingly. Pay strict attention to your gestures, your timing, and your facial expressions. Become your own critic—a severe critic. This process will definitely do wonders for you. But you must develop the attitude of never being satisfied with yourself. The moment you are, the party's over.

The egotist never feels the need to do things of this

nature. He's satisfied with what he has and how good he is. And, invariably, his success is short-lived. While the person who is good but always strives to be better, continues to attain new heights. That's why someone like Jack Nicklaus, one of the greatest of professional golfers, will decide to practice for an hour or two right after winning a major tournament. That's why some movie stars are appalled—rather than satisfied—at the screening of rushes of the picture being filmed. They are constantly striving for perfection. When Barbra Streisand saw herself doing her very first TV special on videotape, she was practically in tears. The public loved it but she felt she could have done a lot better. Seeing one's self is only effective if it is done with a critical eye, not an admiring one.

My good friend Red Motley, recently retired chairman of the board of Parade Publications in New York, is a great public speaker who has devoted a large portion of his life to making speeches at sales rallies to help salespeople become more effective. In his famous speech "Nothing Happens Until Somebody Sells Something," he told the following anecdote.

It's just good common sense that you ought to know how you look to the prospect. But I'll bet that 90 percent of the people in this room have no idea how they look to the man across the desk—they've never taken the trouble to find out.

I didn't either . . . until one night when I was taking a refresher course at the Book-Cadillac bar with another salesman. And he said to me, "Motley, you went to college, didn't you?" And I said, "Yes." He said, "You got a Phi Beta Kappa key, didn't you?" I said, "Sure, why?" "Well," he said, "I don't understand why you insist on making people believe you're a tough guy and that you had no education." I said, "What do you mean?" He said, "You talk out of the corner of your mouth."

"I do not."

"You do, too."

"I do not."

"You certainly do."

The argument went on far into the night. It was a draw. I woke up the next morning hung over like a weeping willow, but not so hung over that I didn't remember that crack. I didn't believe it. So I went over to see a friend of mine, the advertising manager for the Chrysler Corporation, R. M. Roland, in Detroit. And I said, "Rolly, you're a friend of mine so tell me the truth. Do I talk out of the corner of my mouth?" He said, "You certainly do and I've often wondered why."

Well, Mrs. Motley and the kids were in

hysterics for months while the old man practiced his pitch in front of a mirror. But I don't talk out of the corner of my mouth anymore.

I found out one other thing, too. If I could keep on the rails with that funny-looking puss staring back at me out of a mirror, not even the stoniest-faced buyer could throw me off the track.

Obviously, to speak impressively and to put yourself across effectively, it is imperative that you know how you look to others while speaking. Only then can you make whatever adjustments may be necessary. And in addition to the mirror test, there are other more sophisticated possibilities. Videotape is one. If you can arrange to be videotaped, watching yourself during the playback will be most revealing. Still another medium is the home-movie camera that also records sound—a terrific method of self-evaluation.

Let's assume that you are scheduled for an interview for a very important job. How you come across at that first interview will most likely determine whether you get the job—or get further consideration. You certainly want to put your best foot forward. Imagine how well you could prepare yourself for such an interview if you did some role-playing with a friend or member of your family while it was taped or filmed. You could then screen it several times, critique it, and vastly improve upon how you come across. Look at the advantage you'll have over the interviewer. It will be his first interview with you, but your third or fourth with him. You will have been over that road before and you're well prepared with experience and confidence as a side benefit.

When Curt Gowdy resigned as sportscaster on a local radio and television station for the Boston Red Sox, he went on to do nationally televised network sports events. There was a scramble for the job opening he left behind. The station interviewed no one. They asked applicants to submit videotapes of themselves in action. And why not? They could go over them several times, pit one against another, and finally come up with the best possible person for the job. The tapes revealed not only how well applicants spoke but also how they looked . . . on the tube.

How do you look and sound to people? If you don't know, start finding out.

3
Bad Habits in Speaking

A bachelor salesman living in a noisy apartment building told me that he had trouble going to sleep at night and this was affecting his work. I gave him a recording of an egotist who thought he was a good speaker. It contained a forty-minute speech on salesmanship (twenty minutes on each side) and it was a monotone from beginning to end. I told him to listen to it at bedtime with the lights out. Two weeks later he stopped in to tell me that it worked "like a charm." He said, "I've used it every night and I have yet to hear side two."

THE MONOTONE

Nothing is more deadly than having to listen to someone who speaks in a monotone. Probably the greatest single reason that most speakers are boring is that they drone on without any variation in their speech pattern. Since this conveys the idea that the speaker himself isn't interested in what he is saying, this fault is death to effective communication—in business or anywhere else.

In our sales training classes at the Lacy Institute, we go out of our way to make each and every lecture stimulating. It not only makes learning more interesting for those attending but it actually charges them up so they are eager to put what they're learning into practice. Almost invariably a young sales trainee will linger after class to tell us how enjoyable it was. And just as invariably, he will follow this up by saying, "If only the lectures at college had been like this." Most recent college graduates, who still remember those professors whose lectures seemed to last for an eternity, will tell you that cutting classes is usually due to the monotone delivery of the teacher. It's almost torture to have to sit for an hour and listen to a monotonous sound consisting of words that run into each other. It is no different in general conversation. Single out boring people and you will realize that the reason they are boring is very often because they speak in a monotone. People who have a deviated septum, causing them to constantly speak nasally, tend to be boring. This is because the nasal sounds they make are usually constant in tone or pitch and thus a monotone is produced.

Some will argue that the tone quality of the speaking voice is something we are born with—and while it is melodious with some, it may well not be so with others. This is quite true. But speaking in a monotone is not directly related to one's tone quality but rather to one's poor inflection—failure to vary the pitch of the voice.

This point can be easily proven. A fan with a noisy motor won't keep you awake on a warm night. At first you are convinced that it will. But soon you fall asleep without much problem. The reason? The noise is constant and at the same pitch. It's a monotone, so it puts you to sleep. The air conditioner has the same effect, except that if it has a thermostat, the pitch will change when the compressor cuts in and will hamper your departure to slumberland. The monotone has been broken. Much like when you doze off while watching television. The volume and tone remain constant and, depending on how tired you are, you begin to doze. Then a commercial comes on, which is usually much louder than the regular programming, and you awake with a start. The monotone has been broken.

As you can see, therefore, to avoid speaking in a

monotone is very easy. All you have to do is vary the pitch. And you can do this very naturally if you make an effort to speak *enthusiastically* when the subject warrants it and to return to normal tones when it does not.

In the latter case, however, you still can avoid a monotone by using inflection. For instance, let's examine the following sentence.

I hope that I never have to go through such a horrible experience again.

This is the type of sentence that would normally be spoken in a monotone. The person speaking is relating a bad experience; the mood is sad and there's nothing to be enthusiastic about. However, if emphasis is placed on the strong words that aptly describe the speaker's feelings, a substantial amount of inflection can be produced and the monotone is avoided. The same sentence would, therefore, be spoken as follows.

I hope that I *NNNever* have to go through such a *HORRible* experience again.

The formula to avoid monotone delivery can be reduced to very simple terms.

1. Whenever possible, speak enthusiastically. (If you can transmit your enthusiasm to the

person with whom you are speaking, you have put yourself across most effectively.)

2. When enthusiasm per se is out of place, make certain that the strong words are properly emphasized. (Develop the constant awareness of the types of words being used. Once this has been achieved the placing of emphasis on the strong ones becomes almost automatic.)

It's been said that an old form of Chinese torture was to place a person in solitary confinement, in the dark, listening to slowly dripping water. The monotony of the dripping water was the worst aspect. If something monotonous is equated with torture, the message is loud and clear. If, even on occasion, you speak in a monotone—stop! You are *torturing* your listeners.

BAD SPEECH HABITS ARE MOST ANNOYING

Think about the last time that you were totally irritated by someone whose speech was infested with *ers* and *ahs* and the pauses to accommodate them. You felt like saying, "Will you please come out with what you're trying to say?" But you couldn't be that rude. You suffered through it. And your irritating friend wasn't even aware of this habit—a very bad habit.

The following is from a tape of a radio talk show. The talkmaster was getting public opinion on pending gun-control legislation. A man called in and said (please read aloud for maximum impact),

> Hi . . . ah . . . how are you? Fine. Ah . . . I'd like to . . . ah . . . add my . . . ah . . . two cents to this . . . ah . . . gun-control law . . . ah . . . you've been talking about. Ah . . . it seems to me . . . ah . . . that . . . ah . . . any adult . . . ah . . . who is . . . ah . . . say . . . ah . . . twenty- one or over . . . ah . . . should be able to . . . ah . . . get a permit and . . . ah . . . own a gun . . . ah . . . small or large. Ah . . . after all . . . ah . . . do you realize that . . . ah . . . more people are . . . ah . . . killed each year by automobiles . . . ah . . . than by . . . ah . . . guns? To me . . . ah . . . it's absolutely . . . ah . . . crazy to . . . ah . . . limit the gun permits . . . ah . . . to people . . . ah . . . who have a . . . ah . . . valid reason only . . . ah . . . and deny all others. Ah . . . you certainly don't . . . ah . . . have to have . . . ah . . , a valid reason for . . . ah . . . owning or . . . ah . . . driving a car. Yet . . . ah . . . a seventeen-year-old . . . ah . . . can get behind the . . . ah . . . wheel of a car and . . . ah . . . kill a

few people . . . ah . . . the very first day. Ah . . . ah . . . these lawmakers just don't . . . ah . . . use their heads. I say . . . ah . . . let's look at the . . . ah . . . statistics of . . . ah . . . things like this . . . ah . . . first and . . . ah . . . then arrive at conclusions about . . . ah . . . a gun-control . . . ah . . . law. Suppose . . .

At this point the talkmaster couldn't stand it any longer. The agony was too much for him and the radio audience. So he politely dismissed him by saying, "Well, sir, you've made your point and we must move along. Thank you for calling." He had already pressed the button. There was no way in which he could let this caller strain through another sentence on the air.

Let's examine what happened here. The caller had used 204 words to make his point. Of these, 48 were *ahs*. Almost every fourth word was an *ah* with a pause before and after it. To have to listen to him was painful. Imagine this person at a job interview. How do you think he would come across? If only someone would sit him down and make him listen to himself on tape. He might then realize that this horrible speech habit is hampering him every time he opens his mouth.

How do *you* sound on tape? Have you ever taken the trouble to find out? If you haven't, and many individuals have not, we suggest you place this assignment very high on your things-to-do list. You probably already own a tape recorder, but you may never have thought about this possible use for it. If that's the case, here is a good way to get a natural recording of how you really speak. With adhesive or cellophane tape, attach the recorder microphone as close as possible to the mouthpiece of your telephone. Then phone a friend of yours and as soon as he or she answers, press the "record" button. *Don't* tell the other party that you are recording your portion of the conversation. Keep the call as natural as possible. Once you get involved in the conversation you will soon forget that you are recording yourself and you will speak in your own natural fashion. When you play back the tape, be very critical of yourself. Forget your ego. Place yourself in the shoes of a listener and determine if the voice is pleasing to the ear, if there is enough inflection, and if there are any bad speech habits that need to be corrected.

If you don't own a tape recorder, buy one. Many cassette types sell for under thirty dollars. It will be one of the best investments you ever made. Just think, every time you are readying yourself for an important presentation, an interview, a speech, an oral bid for a raise, you can first record it at home. Then, by listening and refining, you will make certain that you come across in the best possible way.

Once you develop the technique of taping yourself, be sure to go through this exercise every so often. Our speaking habits are so subject to change that one can never rest assured that all is well. It is so easy to pick up words and phrases from others, some good, some bad, without even realizing it. Accents and drawls are catchy. Mispronounced words are sometimes adopted unknowingly. The perils are many.

We must all become keenly aware of our susceptibility to bad speaking habits. Some of these habits are more contagious than many of the dread diseases. They creep into our speech almost instantly and then they linger indefinitely or until detected (for us by others). In the process, the damage that is done can be devastating. I'm sure you have conversed with people whose speech pattern resembles the following:

> Jack...you understand? And...okay?
> Then...okay? And...you understand?

This type of conversationalist is almost saying to you, "Listen, stupid, am I going slow enough for you?" And you resent being talked to in this fashion. In fact, after a while you begin to count the *you understands and the okays*. When this happens you're not even listening to what else is in between. What's more, you don't care.

Also annoying is the person who ends each sentence with *right?* And then, "..., right?" Doubly annoying is the pause that comes after each *right*. During that pause you're supposed to register agreement by either nodding or squeezing in your own *right*. Of course, you could throw in a *wrong*, but that upsets the whole conversation. This type of person is thrown for a loss. It could even start an argument. But you don't want to be rude so you end up weathering the storm.

The word *like* is still another offender. Somehow, a few years ago, it was adopted as an "in" colloquial term by teenagers. Almost overnight it spread to all age groups. Its use was, and still is, hard to rationalize. Here's a typical sentence as uttered by a person with the *like* affliction:

> So I said to him, like, I know I don't have, like, the right experience for this job, but I do have, like, two years of training that, like, could be considered as an equivalent. And he said, like, we'll keep your resumé on file and, like, if other openings come up, like, in a month or two, we'll, like, get in touch with you.

Hard to read, isn't it? Even harder to have to listen to it. Clearly, the word *like* is sometimes used as a substitute for *ers* and *ahs*. Its constant use is a bad habit. It may be a fill-in for dead-air spots in one's speech, but its nuisance value is quite obvious.

THE RUT SOME PEOPLE GET INTO

One of the reasons (and perhaps the major one) that people get into a rut using *likes, ers,* and *ahs* is because there is a subconscious tendency to avoid pauses between words or phrases and to fill them in with *something.* That *something* becomes *anything* and remains that way for long periods of time, if not indefinitely. The truth of the matter is that it is much less annoying to live through a pause than to listen to repetitive insertions born of bad speech habits. Actually, there is nothing wrong with a slight pause while the computer in your cranium selects the proper words and phrases with which to speak your thoughts. In fact, it is a very natural thing. That's how, on radio, you can tell if someone is speaking extemporaneously or reading from a script. The latter flows almost too smoothly. There are no pauses.

Some very effective public speakers use the pause for effect. After having made a very strong or controversial point, they pause, as if to give the audience a chance to absorb what's just been said. Others will pause just before a hard-to-pronounce word to ensure that it comes out properly. Still others will pause just before delivering a punch line or revealing the surprise ending to a story.

It adds impact. In all of these instances, as well as in others, the pause is not annoying. It is accepted as a natural thing to do.

Insurance companies place tremendous emphasis on the telephone techniques of the salespeople. After all, much of the prospecting is done via phone calls through which appointments are set up for personal presentations. One company had a speech specialist, in collaboration with a psychologist, develop a telephone script for the sales staff. It was designed to transmit warmth and credibility as well as develop enough interest to induce the listener to agree to an appointment. I saw a copy of it. The most intriguing aspect of the script was that the places where the salesperson was to pause were very clearly marked "/pause/." There were many pauses, at strategic positions, all inserted to make the salesperson sound more natural. The company reasoned that when your privacy is invaded by a soliciting phone call, it would be adding insult to injury to also subject you to a canned sales pitch.

If we accept the premise, therefore, that pauses are natural, then we should stop being concerned over what little dead air they produce. Instead, we should pay strict attention to the many and varied fill-ins that are heard on a daily basis and make certain that they have not crept into our style of speaking. And this awareness has to be practiced constantly because one never knows when a new fill-in will come into vogue, dragging millions into its rut.

The latest to rear its ugly head seems to be the abrasive expression *ya know*. The growth of the *ya know* fraternity must be phenomenal. Everywhere you go you are apt to encounter someone in the *ya know* rut. And the expression has lost its original meaning completely. While you are being told something entirely unknown to you, the *ya knows* are inserted after every third or fourth word. Ridiculous, in more ways than one.

Shaking the *ya know* habit must be a monumental task, judging by how quickly some people adopt it and how deeply it influences their manner of speaking.

During a recent sales seminar one of the salespeople in attendance requested permission to relate one of his experiences. He told a marvelous marketing story with a sad ending. The product didn't sell. When he was through I complimented him for remembering all of the details and thanked him for sharing this knowledge with all who were present. Then I said, "Would you believe, Bill, that I counted over forty *ya knows* while you were speaking? Have you ever tried to get rid of this habit?" His answer was a classic. He said, "Ya know, I'm very aware that I've picked up this, ya know, habit, but, ya know, one of these days I'll get rid of it. Ya know, I used to be what you call, ya know, a chain smoker. Well, ya know, when I made up my mind, ya know, I stopped.

And soon, ya know, I'm going to stop, ya know, saying ya know."

The group roared with laughter and Bill joined them. It was funny for the moment. But consider this. A salesman with the *ya know* habit is much more like the cab driver with worn-out shock absorbers in his aging cab. He gets you there but the ride is annoyingly bumpy.

4
About
Your Vocabulary

Far too many people think that they can impress others with their flashy use of a superb vocabulary. (That is, superb to the speaker, not to the listener.) Yet the impressive speaker is one who realizes that this theory is a total misconception. In some instances with some listeners even the word *misconception* is too big. It falls in the category of the so-called thirty-five-cent words.

MISCONCEPTIONS

The tendency to use big, unusual, and rarely used words can be traced to a variety of impulses. Certainly it is not sparked when children are learning the English language in the classroom. Simplicity of language is the theme there. Grammar is in the spotlight. Yet, in rare instances, because even teachers are human, the classroom could have been the site where the seed was originally planted. To this day I can recall when my seventh-grade teacher was scolding a boy in my class. He had passed in an assignment that was well written but contained an abundance of misspelled words. The teacher was disgusted. With an angry voice she said, "If your rewrite has one single spelling mistake, you'll cause me to excoriate you with bitter invective." The boy burst out laughing. Who understood what that meant? And now the teacher was boiling. So she went to the blackboard, wrote out the words *excoriate* and *invective,* and told us we had to write ten sentences containing these words for homework. This forced all of us to look them up. Well, the next day every member of the class was going out of the way to use these words in regular conversation. It was all very amusing but fortunately it died out in a few days. One girl, however, went back to the dictionary and found a carload of other words that nobody had ever heard or used. Every day she would spring one or two more on us. She soon ceased to be funny. Before long she became downright irritating. Heaven only knows if she's still at it as an adult. I hope she has seen the light.

Other people develop this tendency by reading articles or columns in magazines and newspapers that offer vocabulary training. They usually carry a title, in bold-faced type, such as, "Increase Your Word Power" or "Improve Your Vocabulary" or "Know Your Language." If you examine the contents of these "educational" gems, you'll find the most far out, least-used words imaginable. Each successive article or column must get more difficult for the writers, who seem to scrape the bottom of the barrel. One of them, recently, contained the word *parsimony*. Don't bother to look it up.

This is not to say that the thirst for a thorough knowledge of the English language and the words in it should not be satisfied. The point being made here is simply that there is certainly no harm in being interested in, and learning, the unusual and rarely used words in our language. Just don't adopt them for everyday use in speaking with others. Because, more often than not, people won't ask you what you mean, for fear that they are showing their stupidity. Instead, they let you go on and on without really understanding what you're saying.

NEVER TALK ABOVE THEIR HEADS

To speak above the absorbing capacity of listeners is to lose them. The most complex subject can be discussed with people who are not at all knowledgeable on the matter. It's merely a case of replacing the technical or sophisticated words and phrases with language that the average individual can understand.

Recently the chief newscaster of a television station was joined on the air by a pleasant fellow who sat beside him and shared the reporting duties. To publicize the formation of this news team, both Tom and Tony went out to various parts of the city with a camera crew to film short interviews with people at their work. Then they aired these on television to attract further attention to their newscasts. The interviews were quite informal. Tom would walk up to a construction worker, shake hands as he introduced himself, and then say, "I'd like you to meet Tony Smith. He will be coanchoring with me on the six o'clock news." Come on, now, how many people would know what *coanchoring* means? Construction worker, fruit peddler, policeman—they all had the same expression on their faces as the camera zoomed in for a close-up. It was the smiling expression that says, "I wish I knew what in hell you're talking about." But Tom and Tony, it was obvious, couldn't see the forest for the trees.

You may think that this point is being overly emphasized, but many people who should have known better have committed this sin over the years. Certainly we should expect that politicians, who always want to reach the masses, would take every precaution to make certain that they not talk over the people's heads. But that has not always been so. Back when Franklin D. Roosevelt was president, there was no television. But FDR was a strong believer in communicating with the people, so he started his fireside chats on radio. It was a great idea, for which he was applauded. But there was one problem, He had and used a superb vocabulary. Half the time the masses weren't sure of just what he was saying.

When Adlai Stevenson was running for president, his chances were considered excellent. He had the image of a true statesman. He had the following, the charm, and certainly the intellect that could win him the election. At one point in his campaign he went on a whistle-stop tour through a large number of states. The train would stop at small railroad stations where large crowds had gathered. From the decorated platform of the observation car, Stevenson would make his pitch to the people. But his humor was so subtle that they didn't laugh at the right places. The great promises he made didn't quite come across. His language was too sophisticated for the average American, who applauded him to be polite but didn't understand him. Stevenson lost. You would think his advisers could have detected the problem.

When Richard Nixon was struggling with the problem of withdrawing troops from Vietnam, he appeared on television to transmit his reasoning to the people. During the speech he said, "The *precipitous* withdrawal of troops. . . ." Twice more during the speech he used the word *precipitous*, among others that were foreign to the average American. This was communicating with the masses?

During a television newscast on one of the major networks, the Washington correspondent was interviewing a member of Congress who said that he felt relieved that "the President was being so pragmatic." At the end of the interview the correspondent faced the camera to sum up what had been said, and he, too, used the word *pragmatic*. Of the millions of Americans watching, how many do you suppose know and use the word *pragmatic*. What happened to the more everyday word—*realistic*.

WHOM ARE YOU TRYING TO IMPRESS?

We're dealing with the subject of impressive speaking. Impressive to whom? The listener, obviously. The widespread tendency to impress ourselves by inflicting our vocabulary on others is actually a great way to lose points. It's essential never to lose sight of the danger of making our listeners feel inadequate and uncomfortable. You have heard the expression "a little knowledge is a dangerous thing." Well, that certainly applies here.

Just let a person realize that he knows more about something than his listeners and he's off. Not only will such an "expert" dominate the conversation but he'll also manage to bring in as many technical terms as possible. The sad part is that people who are afflicted with this problem actually expect everyone to listen in awe. They are unaware that those listening are annoyed at being shown how little they know about the subject at hand.

Not long ago I was invited to speak at a convention of wholesale druggists. As I mingled with a number of them during the cocktail party it was obvious that most of the conversations were related to their industry. And rightly so. This is what all of them had in common. However, when I joined one particular group of twelve men, there was one individual who had the floor. He had recently completed a correspondence course on radio and TV repairing and was inflicting a barrage of technical terms on everybody in the group. In a matter of minutes the group began to shrink. One by one the thoroughly bored druggists would slowly slip away to join another group where, hopefully, the conversation would be more interesting. I stayed, mainly because I was completely amazed at just how unaware this self-made technician was of his ego. I had to see how long it would take for him to come back to earth. He never did. How unfortunate. He spoke well, too. He was definitely a good communicator. At the age of about forty, however, he still hadn't learned what impresses listeners and what bores them.

YOUR EGO CAN WORK AGAINST YOU

A controlled ego is helpful for the development of confidence as well as other personality traits. But it must be *completely* controlled. Without an ego, for example, a salesperson rarely succeeds. The same can also be said of a public speaker. Yet, in both cases, if the ego gets out of hand, it works against you.

One of the basic qualifications of good salespeople is that they must know their product or service as thoroughly as possible. How can they sell something to others if they can't explain it in detail. As a result companies spend much time and money in making certain that they provide the sales force with all the product knowledge necessary, and then some. What they usually fail to do, however, is to warn each salesperson against insisting on giving the "whole dose" to every prospect they approach. And when this little detail is left to the salesperson to deal with, the result is directly proportional to that individual's ego—as in the case of the new car salesman who approached a well-groomed man looking over a sporty model on the showroom floor. After answering a question or two about optional equipment available, he went into a masterful and complete explanation of the car's fuel injection system. The prospective buyer didn't understand one word of it but there was never a letup. He was even shown detailed diagrams in a technical brochure. The prospect only wanted to know two things. What did it cost and would it get him where he wanted to go, inexpensively? He left without buying.

The public speaker can lose his audience in the very same way—because of his ego. How well I recall a cold, snowy day in January in Hartford, Connecticut. It was 8:30 A.M. and the beginning of a two-day sales seminar that I was about to conduct for a good-sized company. The president of the company was on hand and asked for the opportunity to say a few words to the group. Naturally, the request was granted. As he held on to the lectern he smiled at the group and said, "I had planned on spending some time here for this seminar but I decided to go to Florida instead. In fact, I'll be taking off in a little over an hour from now, before I get snowed in with the rest of you. I'll think of you after lunch when I'm soaking up the warm sun on the golf course. After all, why do you think we set up a branch office in Florida? I told my secretary to make reservations for me to go to Florida every time a snowstorm has been forecast this winter, ha, ha, ha!" It was all very funny—but only to him. Talk about turning off a group of people with only a few sentences.

All he could think of was *himself*. Not once did the thought enter his mind that his people would have to stay in the cold north country because they didn't enjoy his privileges. He certainly didn't ask himself, "What can I do for this audience?" He simply did something for himself, for his own ego.

Was he unusual? Not at all. If you will listen carefully when in conversation with others, you'll find that the ego in people is ever-present and rarely well-controlled. They just have to tell you what *they* think, where *they* went, what *they* did. And all of this comes out without even a proper opening for the subject. Such as when you meet Jack, whom you haven't seen for a few weeks, and you say, "Hi, Jack, nice to see you." And he responds, "Just got back from Puerto Rico." Now, you didn't ask where he's been, but he's going to tell you about it and in detail. He's still on cloud nine. The glow from his vacation is still with him. He will inflict this on everybody he meets for at least the next two weeks. His ego is not in control.

Are there any guidelines to be followed in controlling one's ego? There certainly are. If you will follow two simple rules, you will find it very easy to keep your ego in check.

1. Never talk about yourself boastfully.
2. Show a strong interest in people by discussing matters related to them rather than yourself.

Couple these two rules with the other suggestions on impressive speaking covered in this book and your ego will not interfere when you are engaged in oral communication. Furthermore, we can sum up the ego problem this way. Your ego makes you want to speak well so that people are properly impressed and will appreciate you more. That's understandable. Yet everything you say and how you say it should be planned and executed with the listener in mind. So it's okay to enjoy yourself through your speaking ability, but just make sure the listener is *also* enjoying what's going on. In fact, if the listener is enjoying what you're saying even more than you are—you've succeeded.

5
Nervous Tension Affects Speech

You have most likely found that there are some days when you seem to do everything right. You say the right thing at the right time in the right way. You feel secure, confident, happy. You feel able to convince anyone of anything. Then you have days that are just the opposite. You find yourself saying the wrong thing at the wrong time in the wrong way. You get into misunderstandings without even trying. Everything backfires. You can't convince anyone of anything. Bewildering, isn't it?

THERE IS SOME NERVOUS TENSION IN ALL OF US

Well, the reason is nervous tension. It's a condition from which all normal individuals suffer in varying degrees on certain days. The amount of tension is directly proportional to what we are doing and what we are thinking. Rushing to make a train or plane, driving a car on a foggy night, changing a tire on a busy highway can all cause tension. The conditions are such that abnormal pressure has been placed on us and nervous tension results. A golfer, for instance, at the end of a four-hour round at his favorite course may be somewhat tired from walking but he's thoroughly relaxed. He enjoyed himself. But place him in a highly competitive tournament on the very same course and see what happens. By the time he has finished the round he's a nervous wreck. He's exhausted. Win or lose, the pressure is difficult to withstand. It may all be over but he's still expressing dissatisfaction with himself over the ten-inch putt he missed way back on the second hole (because of nervous tension).

Some people, due to severe stress conditions, will become so tense that they black out mentally and lose all sense of direction. Some years ago a football player of All-America caliber was playing in a Rose Bowl game.

When an opposing player fumbled the ball, he recovered it and began to run with it (a perfectly legal reaction). But he became so tense that he took off toward the wrong goal line. One of his teammates, who was much less tense, overtook and tackled him on his five-yard line—otherwise he would have scored for the opposing team.

When you are relaxed and free from nervous tension you achieve coordination of mind and muscle. As a result, you can apply your maximum power with a minimum of effort. One of the chief characteristics of champions in any activity is their ability to relax and do their best work when the pressure is the greatest.

A strange fact about nervous tension is that while it can be such a destructive force, the ability to control it can be tremendously helpful. For example, in many cultures childbirth is often associated with extreme pain. The end result is glorious, but the delivery can be frightening. Yet, after over seven hundred carefully recorded cases of *painless* childbirth, Dr. Grantly Read, a London obstetrician, had this to say. "No drugs of any kind were used. Just remove the tension and substitute relaxation and childbirth can be painless."

Since tension affects us in every way imaginable, it certainly affects our ability to speak well under pressure. The wrong words come out or, sometimes, no words at all, depending on the severity of the situation. If someone took you by the hand, led you through a door onto the stage of an auditorium, and introduced you to an audience of a thousand people to make a short speech, what would happen? Your hands would immediately begin to perspire, hundreds of butterflies would begin to flutter in your stomach, and your knees would insist on buckling. Why? Because you have been suddenly placed in an unusual stress situation. You're not accustomed to having a sea of faces staring at you while waiting for the next word to come out. Your nervous tension is at an all-time high and you find it difficult to control because you cannot control it with your will. How do you think your voice would sound? How interesting would you be to the audience?

In the process of conducting sales seminars I always try to include some role playing. One attendee will act as the buyer and another as the sales representative attempting to sell the product or services of the company concerned. As many such skits as possible are set up, using different people. After each skit, constructive critiques are held.

Now, you would think that salespeople who are engaged in selling a particular product or service *on a daily basis* could come forward and easily deliver a sales presentation that would flow like wine. After all, think of how many times a day they've done this, every day. Well, forget it. That's hardly the case. First of all, I rarely get volunteers. I have to call upon people and assign them a role to play—which they accept most reluctantly. Some even dread the whole idea. And the presentations they make are usually far from professional in quality. Why? Because they become "too nervous" and "too tense." To make a sales presentation before an audience is nerve-shattering. To make it before a group of peers is mortifying. The result is, therefore, far from what most attendees are capable of doing under normal circumstances, when they are much more relaxed, though not completely.

Obviously, to be nervous and tense is bad. To be saddled with nervous tension and have to speak is worse. That's why it's important to learn how to control tension and thereby greatly improve our speaking abilities. Let's further understand the causes, however, and then we'll get into the cure.

PSYCHOLOGICAL REASONS FOR TENSION

Although many people may not be willing to admit it, a major cause for their nervous tension is lack of confidence. It's a mental state that raises havoc, inwardly, with more people than we realize. Mistakenly we assume that those who are afflicted with a lack of confidence are only those who look and act like introverts. Forget it. Not so. A substantial number of poised, seemingly extroverted individuals are constantly affected by a serious lack of confidence. They try hard not to show it. They strive to produce the effect of possessing a very outgoing personality but the amount of nervous tension they are experiencing in the process is tremendous. They may feel inferior to others or ill-equipped for a task or uncomfortable with strangers. Whatever the reason, the tension is there and it mounts as long as certain conditions exist.

Such tension can be hidden to a great extent but it invariably shows up when the person begins to speak. The voice may quiver or sound raspy or even squeaky. The words are hard to come by or they run together. And all this because the tension is so hard to control.

I discussed this recently with a director of personnel of a large company. After years of personnel work he has come to the conclusion that 99 percent of those who are being interviewed for a job are extremely nervous and tense. In fact, it is understood by all interviewers that certain allowances must be made for this. However, he said, if an applicant is so tense that making sense becomes a problem, one just has to conclude that such a person would only be another problem employee.

Many people rationalize that psychological tension only occurs when one is faced with doing something new and different. The truth is, however, that every single day offers something different. No matter how rigid the daily routine, something unusual is bound to come about. And depending on its irritating effect, tension can and usually does result.

Worry also causes considerable tension in people. All of us have problems of varying magnitudes and we tend to worry about them almost constantly. We know full well that we should be thinking of ways to solve them but we just don't. Instead we worry to such a degree that the problems loom greater than they actually are. And tension mounts even higher. Ever notice how a worried person speaks? There is no life in the voice, no enthusiasm. A boring monotone is a certainty.

PHYSIOLOGICAL REASONS FOR TENSION

In addition to the psychological reasons for nervous tension, there are physiological reasons over which we have no control. To understand them requires a brief explanation of our physical makeup as it pertains to this subject.

The diaphragm is one of the largest muscles in our body. It is shaped like an opened umbrella and separates the chest cavity from the abdominal cavity. It is an involuntary muscle, which means that we have absolutely no control over it. When we want to flex our fingers or move our arms, we just decide to do so and the desired action follows. Not so with the diaphragm. We simply cannot control it. In fact, when the diaphragm goes into spasm it produces hiccups, and no matter how many sips of water we take or how many paper bags we breathe into, the condition will not subside. When the diaphragm decides to relax, and not until then, will the hiccups go away.

When we are lying down the diaphragm is relaxed. But during the hours that we are sitting or standing, there is constant tension on the diaphragm. All of the abdominal organs, the stomach, pancreas, intestines, liver, and others are exerting a downward pull and the diaphragm compensates by tightening up.

Because of this constant tension on the diaphragm and because this muscle is associated with the involuntary nervous system, we experience tension throughout the entire body. It travels via the involuntary nervous system to every conceivable part of the body, including the throat and the vocal cords. As the day progresses the tension increases. We start off each day with a relaxed diaphragm because we have been lying down all night. (That's why our respirations per minute decrease and we breathe more deeply while we're sleeping. The diaphragm is completely relaxed.) However, as soon as we assume an upright position, the tension begins and increases as we become more tired. It's all downhill until bedtime.

Then, as if this whole picture weren't gloomy enough, there is another problem which complicates matters even more.

Since we don't breathe deeply enough, we never have an overabundance of oxygen throughout the body. Perhaps you will be surprised to learn that the lower 20 percent of our lungs have never seen any good, clean oxygen. Whenever an autopsy is performed, there is proof of this by the color of the lungs in the lower area. We are all as lazy as we dare to be, and this includes our breathing habits. We breathe in just enough oxygen to stay alive and no more.

Oxygen is the energizing element of the body and every single tissue requires it. As the day progresses, we expend more and more energy and the body requires more oxygen—but it doesn't get it. The result? General tiredness. By four o'clock in the afternoon we seem to be "dragging." Some people begin to yawn. Most people are certain to start yawning by early evening. By that time not only has tiredness caught up with them but the additional strain of digesting the largest meal of the day has also been placed on the body. More oxygen is needed and it just isn't forthcoming.

This general fatigue further increases nervous tension. That's why people tend to lose their tempers more easily towards the end of the day. Note also that, by evening, the voice is not as low or as resonant as it was in early morning. In fact it gets somewhat scratchy, unclear, and in some cases, downright irritating to the ear of a listener.

All this may sound frustrating to deal with, but don't despair. There *is* a solution. It all revolves around your willingness to learn how to relieve the constant tension on the diaphragm while at the same time greatly increasing your intake of oxygen.

6
Relieving Physical Tension

Tension is something all of us experience at one time or another. Learning to cope with it effectively is vital if you want to learn to talk your way to success. Only when you are relaxed and at ease do you communicate with the kind of confidence necessary for business success. Happily, you don't need complicated relaxation techniques or tranquilizers to relieve tension. By using the simple breathing technique presented here, you can virtually wipe out tension, greatly increase your energy, feel better, and sound better—all in a matter of minutes. The process through which you do all this is called diaphragmatic breathing. It is a method of breathing and breath control that will pay you huge dividends for the rest of your life.

Remember your school gym teacher who would bellow: "Okay, now it's time for some deep breathing exercises. Inhale—chest out, stomach in—exhale. Again, chest out, stomach in, inhale, exhale." Actually, this was a great way to expand the chest, inflate the lungs to maximum capacity, and take in additional oxygen. However, it did absolutely nothing in the way of relieving tension. In fact, it increased it.

Prove this to yourself right now. Place your left hand on your chest and your right hand on your waist. Now inhale. Observe how much your chest actually rises and to what degree your stomach is pulled in. Now exhale. Note that the chest goes down to normal position and the stomach comes out. Now inhale just once more, but this time hold your breath as long as you possibly can. Note how you get a feeling of tenseness in the small of your back. If the breath is held long enough, the feeling turns into an actual pain. This is due to muscular tension, which in turn creates nervous tension. Now you can see how this type of deep breathing is actually creating more tension on the diaphragm rather than relaxing it.

Diaphragmatic breathing has the opposite effect. It relaxes the diaphragm, puts more oxygen in your blood stream, and makes your voice more resonant. Here is how you take a diaphragmatic breath. As you inhale, make a special effort to leave the chest where it is. Do not raise or attempt to push it out. Place your left hand on it and make sure it stays in place. Then place your right hand on your stomach. Now, as you inhale air, push your stomach out. If your hand moves forward, you'll know that you are pushing it out. Do this a few times to get used to the method. Take in as much air as you can. You may experience a little dizziness. If so, just stop for a minute and then resume. The dizziness is nothing to worry about. It is caused by your having allowed oxygen to penetrate to the lower cells of your lungs. They have been dormant so long that they house stagnant air. As you clean this out and substitute wholesome, oxygen-laden air, you are apt to get somewhat dizzy.

Repeat this diaphragmatic breathing several times until you can master holding your chest motionless while pushing the stomach out. And push it out as much as you can—the more the better. You want to take in as much air as possible and pushing the stomach out helps you to accomplish this.

You can easily check yourself to make sure you are doing this correctly. Expel all of the air in your lungs and place your hands on your stomach just above your waist. Make sure that the tips of your middle fingers are touching. Now inhale deeply and, as you do, push the stomach out. If the tips of your fingers become separated (about one to two inches apart) you are doing it right.

Do this at least twelve times in a row. You have now mastered the technique known as diaphragmatic breathing, and you have also learned how to relax yourself at will. Your physical power will now increase, your general health will improve, and whenever you are under pressure, you will know how to get immediate and substantial relief from tension. You will be able to remain calm, think clearly, and handle a situation to your own satisfaction. When you speak while under pressure, your voice will have no tension in it. And all this will do wonders for your confidence and certainly for your ability to put yourself across.

Incidently, if you want to prove to yourself that diaphragmatic breathing offers you complete relaxation, here's a simple test. Spread your hands and fingers lightly across your stomach and laugh heartily. Feel your diaphragm vibrating? That's why people want to laugh whether they realize it or not. Vibrations have a relaxing effect on the diaphragm which in turn produces complete relaxation. And that's also why every year most of the award-winning television shows are comedies.

Do not assume that to get all the benefits of diaphragmatic breathing you have to give up your present breathing method and switch over. By no means. If you were to take only a dozen diaphragmatic breaths spaced out during the course of each day, you would notice the difference this would make in you. However, the more of them that you take each day, the greater the rewards. The trick is to remember to do this. All of us have the greatest of intentions but memory and self-motivation don't always come into play at the right time.

It's important, therefore, that you develop certain helpful reminders.

If you drive your automobile for a substantial portion of each day, you have a built-in reminder. Every time you stop at a red traffic light, take a diaphragmatic breath. All of us use the telephone to a substantial degree. Every time you find yourself dialing a number, take a diaphragmatic breath. You also should do this every time you answer your telephone just before you begin to speak. Since we all seem to open and close a substantial number of doors each day, perhaps every time you find yourself with a doorknob in hand you can take a diaphragmatic breath. And of course, there is no better way to start off each day than by taking a number of them immediately upon arising.

A SURE WAY TO IMPROVE YOUR VOICE

Rich and resonant tones, which carry authority and impressiveness, will be regularly found in the voice once the diaphragm is used during speaking. If you take a diaphragmatic breath and then speak as the exhaled air comes out of your mouth, you will be amazed at the improved sound of your voice. Let's understand that the higher the voice, the more irritating it is to the ear of the listener. Conversely, the lower the voice, the more pleasing it is to the ear. When speaking with air produced by a diaphragmatic breath, the tendency is to lower the voice substantially while making it more resonant.

It is very easy to demonstrate this to yourself. Take a diaphragmatic breath and as the air comes out of your mouth say, "From down below." Take another breath and this time say, "This is from down below." Just one more breath and this time say, "This is from the diaphragm from down below." Go on from there and use sentences of your own choice. Repeat them until they flow easily and resonantly. A good way to master this procedure is to read aloud, making sure that you take a diaphragmatic breath at the beginning of each sentence.

After you've done a reasonable amount of practicing, you will detect a very marked improvement in the sound of your voice. It won't be easy for you to notice it because we don't hear ourselves as others hear us. But you certainly can find out just how much your voice has improved by doing a simple exercise. Face the corner of a room where there are no doors or windows close by. If you stand so that your head is about twelve inches from the point where the walls meet, the sound will bounce back into your ears. Now tense your throat slightly, as you would when you are about to gargle, and say, "This is a tight throat." Now relax completely, take a diaphragmatic breath and as the air comes out of your mouth say, "This is a rich and mellow tone." The difference will astound you.

You realize, of course, that as you master diaphragmatic breathing, you are also gaining deliberate control of your diaphragm. You are doing so indirectly, but there is no question that you are achieving this control. And there's one more thing you can do, unrelated to your breathing, that will greatly help in achieving control of the diaphragm. Lift up your stomach, as high as you can, under your chest and hold it there for a few seconds. Repeat this ten times. Most likely you are now experiencing a slight soreness on your back near the shoulder blades. This is because the muscles that hold up the stomach have become soft and flabby—a major reason why so many people develop a paunch. Incidentally, if you happen to be getting a little thick around the middle this is a quick way to take several inches off your waistline. It won't reduce your weight, however. It merely reduces the extent to which the stomach protrudes by developing the necessary strength in the muscles to hold it up in place.

All of this will greatly improve your voice. And there is nothing magical about it. In fact, none of it is new or unusual. There isn't a TV or radio announcer, comedian or opera star, or anyone who depends on the voice for a living who doesn't know about and regularly use diaphragmatic breathing. It's a must for them and it will be a great plus for you. The average individual, when first exposed to this method, wonders about the possibility of becoming self-conscious. Will pushing the stomach out look rather silly to the listener? Forget it. The listener is always looking at your face. When was the last time that you listened to someone by looking at that person's stomach. Nonsense. It just doesn't work that way. As you master the procedure, you'll do it very rhythmically. Nobody will ever know you're doing it—but they may wonder why you sound resonant and so convincing.

One thing is certain—without realizing it, you will begin to project better. This doesn't mean shouting. It means that because of the lowered pitch of your voice and the developed resonance, you will be easier to understand. You'll come across more clearly and exude confidence and authority while you speak.

You have no idea how important it is to sound good when you speak. Listeners get turned off very quickly when your voice is not just right. They can't tell you why; it's a psychological reaction that borders on, or definitely is, subliminal. Soon after President Lyndon Johnson told the national television audience that he would not be a candidate for reelection, Nicholas Gage, staff reporter of the *Wall Street Journal*, wrote a feature story on voices and voice coaches. Here are some excerpts:

> Now it can be told. Here's why President Johnson decided not to run for reelection. It wasn't because of war or peace. It wasn't because

of tax increases or gold drains. Rather, it was because his voice had become so grating to so many ears that his popularity had fallen dangerously low. He no longer *sounded* like a President. . .

Oral communication experts are also known as voice coaches. These people say that President Johnson's voice is no asset. "The more that people heard his voice the less secure they felt about him. The man just doesn't sound sincere."

What's more, say voice specialists, the major candidates still in the race could use a little toning up, too. All of the candidates have a distraction in their voices, something that breaks the bond with their audiences if they speak for any length of time. . .

Candidates for lesser office, however, are seeking help from voice coaches. Politicians are beginning to realize that without a voice that can be listened to with interest, platform promises can mean very little. . .

One of the first big-name politicians to use a voice coach was John F. Kennedy. During his successful 1960 campaign, his advisors included David Blair McClosky, a baritone who was a professor of voice at the Boston Conservatory of Music.

"He called me when he began to lose his

voice after the strenuous West Virginia primary, and I stayed with him through the election," said Mr. McClosky. "We developed a series of hand signals, and when he was giving a speech he would glance over at me and I would let him know if he was straining too hard or doing something else detrimental to his voice."

McClosky remembers that Robert Kennedy regarded all this with suspicion. "But Jack always found a few minutes each day to work out with me. He knew it was important. . . ."

Voice coaches say that they try to put depth and color into their clients' voices. They teach modulation, inflection and enunciation with a series of special breathing, speaking and relaxing exercises [diaphragmatic breathing].

The importance of a good voice is something everyone should be concerned with, not just politicians. If you simply give it some thought, you'll come up with the names of people you know whom you don't go out of your way to be with. Most likely they are boring. And in most cases they bore you because their conversation is far from interesting, or there is no zip to the way they put their ideas across, or they speak in a monotone. Become more aware of this. As you do, it will help you to avoid making those mistakes. In the process your life will change substantially.

Diaphragmatic breathing has virtually changed the lives of a countless number of people in all walks of life. Athletes, teachers, singers, salespeople, lawyers have all found greater success once they were able to relieve tension and sound better through diaphragmatic breathing. Some years ago, when Frank Fontaine was appearing on the Jackie Gleason television show, his major contribution was his characterization of Crazy Guggenham. One day, in the middle of rehearsing impressions with his voice coach a whole new aspect of entertainment opened up for him. His coach suggested that in addition to doing his impressions from the throat, he should try singing from the diaphragm. In the space of an hour and a half Fontaine discovered and began to develop a fine singing voice. He said, "I couldn't believe it. I said, 'Is it really me?' And then all I could think of was, 'Could I do it again?'" He was given the opportunity to try out his "new voice" on the show after Gleason heard him singing in the dressing room. At the time Gleason was trying to decide whether to hire Tony Bennett or Frank Sinatra to sing on his show. Upon hearing Fontaine singing he decided to forget Bennett and Sinatra. Just another diaphragmatic success story.

HOW PUBLIC SPEAKING BECOMES EASY

Let's face it. Certain people hate to do certain things. Some hate to fly; they fear height. The more they fly the easier it becomes; but they never totally drive away the fear of altitude and that's understandable. Others fear the thought of having to give a speech. When forced into it, they die a thousand deaths. That's understandable, too. So they avoid being placed in that position. There's nothing more satisfying, though, than to have an audience give you a standing ovation. And, speaking from experience, I can tell you that to achieve such high degree of acceptance is not all that hard.

The inexperienced public speaker can attribute most of the butterflies in his stomach to the inborn fear that he's going to do something that will be most embarrassing—like forgetting what to say or losing his poise or his place or his ability to even make a sound. As he looks at the many serious faces staring at him, he gets the feeling that they are all waiting for the first mistake so they can laugh in ridicule. Not so. The truth of the matter is that every person in that room is rooting for the speaker. They relate to him. They *want* him to do well. They *want* to be stimulated. And if he says something funny, they are delighted to laugh. They *want* to be entertained.

If the embryonic public speaker could only keep this in mind before and during his talk, his anxiety and tension would be reduced by at least 50 percent. Then, if he adds the use of diaphragmatic breathing, he's home free. It will all be down to 10 percent.

Believe it or not, tension is greatest *before* the speech. Thinking about the whole ordeal increases the tension by the hour. Then, when the moment is just about to arrive, the speaker usually has to suffer through a long introduction by someone who is also filled with butterflies and the tension reaches its peak. The solution lies in remembering to take a diaphragmatic breath every time you think about the talk you are going to give. And during the introduction, when the audience is listening to the introducer, take a number of successive diaphragmatic breaths. By the time you're on you'll be so relaxed that you'll be able to concentrate on what *you can do for those in the audience* rather than what *they are doing to you.*

7
How to Create Impact

In the process of verbal communication, particularly in business, most of us find ourselves, more often than not, selling our ideas. Listen to the most simple of conversations between any two people and you'll soon detect that one is trying to *convince* the other of something. That's why so many people don't get along with each other. Their views differ and every time they get together one tries to *convince* the other unsuccessfully. They clash on a regular basis. After a number of such clashes they avoid each other. It's the easy way out. To expect that this will ever change is unrealistic. There are certain human tendencies that will exist forever.

But the key word in this observation is *convince*. If indeed we are regularly trying to *convince* someone of something, why not become better at doing so? The art of convincing has, many times, been used as a definition for salesmanship—and rightly so. The convincing process requires skill through the proper use of words and phrases. Above all, it requires *impact*. The more impact you can generate throughout the convincing process, the more successful you are going to be at it.

HAND GESTURES ARE MOST EFFECTIVE

Much of this impact can be produced through hand gestures. Some people use their hands so much when speaking that they invite criticism: "If you tied his hands together he couldn't say a word." But for the most part, people don't use enough hand gestures effectively. In fact, when placed in the position of having to speak to a group, they simply don't know what to do with their hands and it becomes an obsession with them. This is true even with some people who are constantly performing before the public. One would think that, as professional performers, they would no longer be nervous and tense. And they most likely are not. But they just haven't paid enough attention to the use of hand gestures for impact. What they do with their hands becomes a distraction.

When wearing tuxedos, a number of male stars

(Dean Martin in particular) repeatedly adjust their bow ties and their cuff links. In most cases such adjustments are totally unnecessary; they are done unconsciously.

With some singers it's extremely obvious that hand gestures are a problem. They snap their fingers in time with the beat or hold on to a microphone for dear life. Some fold their hands behind their backs and certain male singers simply shove their hands in their pockets and leave them there for the duration of the rendition. Yet, particularly in singing, the hands could be used to make gestures that would greatly enhance the effect the performer is trying to achieve. Take special note, however, of how many of the big stars do use their hands effectively. Opera stars work hard at this and succeed. It's an important part of their training.

I realize that we should be concerning ourselves with speaking rather than singing. Yet the hands come into play in both cases: They either produce substantial impact by the way they are used or they cause distractions that can prove quite annoying. If a speaker is neither articulate nor experienced in the use of gestures, the listener will almost definitely be bored.

Note how many public speakers using a podium assume a bent-forward position with the hands holding on to the sides of the lectern. It's a reassuring position. As long as they can hold on to the lectern they don't have to do anything else with their hands. The problem is solved. And while it's true that certain annoying and

distracting gestures are thereby eliminated, the audience, nevertheless, becomes bored. Looking at a fixed,
motionless human is far from stimulating.

But too many wrong motions can be equally bad.
Red Motley of Parade Publications, to whom we re-
ferred earlier, tells this classic story.

> I remember the last fascinating specimen
> who sat across the desk from me masquerading as
> a salesman. All the time he spoke he kept poking
> his ear with his forefinger. I found myself
> marveling at the durability of the human ear to
> be able to stand that sort of thing—all that goug-
> ing and digging. Then I found myself speculating
> as to what would happen if he ever succeeded in
> breaking through and getting inside that damn
> ear. But the unfortunate, tragic part about it was
> that he didn't know he was doing it. He didn't
> have sense enough to go look in a mirror and find
> out how he looked to the guy on the other side of
> the desk.

Do you know how you look to others while speaking? Have you ever had a chat with yourself before a
mirror? You see, nervousness, in general, is the reason
why many people end up doing silly things with their
hands as they talk. They don't know they're doing this
and don't realize that they are distracting the listener.

Better to concentrate on keeping their hands by their sides or simply folding them to make sure they remain in one place. Unless hand gestures seem and are natural, they will undoubtedly produce the wrong effect.

Some people seem to have an inborn knack for using their hands well when they speak, but a much larger number have to train themselves to use good hand gestures. The correct hand movements can be very important in helping a speaker put a point across. Start noticing the speakers in meetings, presentations, and conferences, and you'll soon discover that the ones who have the most impact know how to use their hands to emphasize significant points. For example, a speaker who says something along the lines of, "This will affect you and you and you," while pointing to various parts of the audience, can give people the feeling that they are being directly singled out. The first step in this process of learning to use your hands well is to eliminate distracting gestures such as fiddling with your glasses, smoothing your hair, and jingling change or keys in your pockets. The next step is to begin to focus on those gestures that heighten what you are saying.

When someone asks you, "Which way did they go?" and you say, "That way," what happens? As you utter those two words, you not only look in that direction but you also point with your index finger. The hand gesture is a natural action that comes about instinctively. If you want to research this phenomenon, simply ask your friends the question, "What is a spiral staircase?" Nine out of ten, as they attempt to describe it, will instinctively make a circling motion with the index finger as it points and travels upwards. Gestures like that are so natural and so emphatic that they never distract. They emphasize what is being said; they ensure clarity and understanding.

If you are not using hand gestures now to any degree, try doing so. Use simple ones at first until you get used to the idea. Soon they will become natural to you. The more you use them, the more effectively you will put yourself across. Just make sure that you guard against the development of annoying gestures similar to those I have described. If you habitually jingle your change in your pocket or play with your keys, stop doing so at once. You will have started the process of self-improvement in this area.

EMPHASIZE IMPORTANT WORDS AND PHRASES

The listener isn't always listening. Let's understand that. Most of us regularly assume that because we are speaking to someone, that person is listening. Far from it. People have problems and they worry about them—almost constantly. When spoken to they may appear to be listening, but their minds are often elsewhere.

It is therefore necessary for the speaker to create impact through the use of words and phrases that will arrest the attention of the listener. If what you are saying has been made interesting by the way in which you are presenting your thoughts, you will *neutralize the mind of the listener.* This means that by arresting the listener's attention, you have automatically driven all other thoughts out of his or her mind.

By placing emphasis on certain words or phrases you do two important things at one time. First, you avoid speaking in a monotone (a deadly sin in itself), and second, you *stimulate* the listener, who in turn decides that what you're saying is most interesting. And when your conversation stimulates people, they are delighted to be with you. They decide that you have a great personality.

How can you create emphasis? Its easy. Simply a case of accepting and using a few obvious rules.

1. SAY IMPORTANT WORDS WITH IMPORTANCE
Certain words deserve particular emphasis when spoken, words like: enth*ooo*siasm, trem*ennnd*ous, h*uuu*ge, *glllor*ious, colo*sssss*al, *deeeel*icious, horrr*rible*, *fffrigh*tening. Such words are basically emphatic, but if not pronounced with the proper emphasis, they will lose most of their impact.

2. USE DESCRIPTIVE ADJECTIVES

By using a well-chosen and highly descriptive adjective just before a commonly used word, you greatly increase the emphasis. Here are some examples: surgically clean, chalk white, fiery red, side-splitting joke, masterful sketch, frightful experience, precise explanation, ferocious temper. Go over these examples for a second time and note how each adjective adds a vivid dimension to what is being described.

3. PAINT WORD PICTURES

Just about all of us were taught in school how to use word pictures. Yet we fail to put such knowledge into play in our everyday conversations. Even when verbal communication is important, such as at an interview, we don't seem to take advantage of this most effective way to produce impact. And word pictures are so easy to come up with if you just get into the habit of choosing specific words that will instantly form a picture in the mind of the listener. Suppose I said to you, "I just saw Jack coming around the corner." Can you visualize Jack coming around the corner? Think about it for a moment. On the other hand, suppose I said, "I just saw Jack coming around the corner on two screeching wheels." Notice how much more easily you are able to visualize the action by the simple addition of only four words. Now you know that Jack was riding, not walking; that he was driving a car; and that he was in an awful hurry. You also learned something about his personality. All this with just four words.

One of the major reasons why we can get so deeply immersed in a book that we just "can't put it down" is because it contains such vivid word pictures that we can actually *see* what the author is describing. We can feel it; we are there.

Take any passage at random from a classic best seller and note how cleverly word pictures are used to activate your imagination. Here's one from Boris Pasternak's *Doctor Zhivago*.

They left the station at dawn. The other tenants were usually asleep at this hour, but one of them, Zevorotnina, incurably fond of organizing *any* social occasion, roused them all, shouting: "Attention! Attention! Comrades! Hurry up! The Gromeko people are going. Come and say goodbye."

They all poured out onto the back porch

(the front door was kept boarded up) and stood at a semicircle as though for a photograph. They yawned and shivered and tugged at the shabby coats they had thrown over their shoulders and stamped about in the huge felt boots they had hastily pulled on over their bare feet.

Markel had already managed to get drunk on some murderous brew he had succeeded in obtaining even in those dry days, and he hung like a corpse over the worn porch railings, which threatened to collapse under him. He insisted on carrying the luggage to the station and was offended when his offer was refused. At last they got rid of him.

It was still dark. The wind had fallen and the snow fell thicker than the night before. Large, fluffy flakes drifted down lazily and hung over the ground, as though hesitating to settle.

By the time they had left the street and reached the Arbat it was lighter. Here the snow came down like a white, slowly descending stage curtain as wide as the street, its fringe swinging around the legs of the passersby so that they lost the sense of moving forward and felt they were marking time.

After reading something so well written, don't you get the urge to meet the author? Wouldn't you be flattered to shake Pasternak's hand? Why? Because you are impressed with him, the way he writes, the personality he projects.

Proper emphasis on what you say and how you say it will help you put both yourself and your ideas across, much like an author does with his writing. The personality you will display will make people decide that being with you is an interesting experience-interesting because they enjoy listening to what you have to say. Basically, that's the major difference between leaders and followers. Leaders work at how to say something so that it sounds totally convincing.

FACIAL EXPRESSIONS

Most of the time a listener is watching your face while you're talking. They say that a good listener focuses directly on your mouth, disregarding the rest of your face. But since *good* listeners are scarce, we will have to assume that the entire face is in complete view. Therefore, *all* of your facial expressions are important.

With facial expressions we transmit much more than we realize. Particularly if you know a person well, you can usually detect telltale signs of tenseness, anger, fear, worry, apprehension, happiness, sorrow, despair, listlessness, quandary, disappointment, surprise. The list must be endless. And what a person says usually coincides with the facial expressions. And that's as it should be: Trying to act happy when you're sad usually doesn't come off as well as you hope. Your facial expressions automatically display your *real* feelings.

Here is one suggestion, however. Try to smile as much as possible. Obviously, if you are discussing a very serious subject, a smile is out of place. But, if the conversation is of average seriousness or definitely on the lighter side, a smile is most desirable. Not a phony smile, but a smile that really comes from liking people. It doesn't matter with whom you're speaking. There is something in everybody you can like. Zero in on that and reflect it with a pleasant smile. When you smile you radiate happiness. A too serious face radiates gloom and there's certainly enough of that around. So, whenever possible and in good taste, make a sincere effort to display a friendly smile while you talk. Television stars are giving you a lesson on this daily in your own home. Notice how announcers, people in talk shows, singers, commentators, sportscasters all smile at you as much as possible. Even newscasters will smile unless they are reporting a catastrophe.

Some facial expressions, however, can very definitely work against you. They either serve to distract the listener or convey a feeling or impression quite foreign to your hopes. Let's take distractions first.

There are some people who speak more with their

eyes than their mouths. They look to the heavens, roll the eyeballs, squint, look to the left and then to the right, blink profusely, close the lids softly or very tightly, wink, stare, show the whites of the eyeballs. Then there are those who do much more with their mouths than speak with them. Between words they use their mouths to display exaggerated expressions of anger, shock, pain, sadness, revenge, or amazement. The listener becomes more enthralled with these mouth movements than with what the speaker is actually saying. Sometimes speakers will lose an audience entirely because of such irritating or even repellent mouth or tongue movements.

We've all seen speakers who have a habit of wetting their lips as they speak. Like any other nervous gesture, this can be very distracting. And in some cases it may actually look as though the speaker is sticking out his tongue at the audience. Hardly a crowd pleaser.

As for the wrong impressions that you can convey through facial expressions, think about the last time you heard someone say, "He looked too anxious." Maybe the face was overexpressive. Then again it may not be expressive enough. Many a sales manager has said, "That person looks too placid to be in sales." You see, certain assumptions are made—some valid, some not—from the very expression on a person's face regardless of whether or not it coincides with what is being said. And some of these assumptions, though wide generalizations, are accepted as fact by most. For example, if a man has the habit of talking out of the side of his mouth, he's labeled a tough guy.

To make sure that your facial expressions are not working against you, have a frank discussion on the subject with someone close to you—someone whose opinion you value and who would have your best interests at heart. You may discover that you need to make a few adjustments in this area. If not, just leave things as they are and continue to act natural when speaking.

TIMING

Have you ever heard a speaker plunge those in the audience into roars of laughter, then move them almost to tears, and shortly thereafter inspire them to great heights? Have you ever witnessed a super salesperson fight through insurmountable resistance and emerge from the presentation with an "impossible" sale? Have you ever wondered what great "secret" power enables these people to sway their listeners with such impact?

The secret is the same in both instances. Many call it enthusiasm. But that's not the complete answer. It is one thing to be enthusiastic and another to be able to transmit your enthusiasm to the people you want to influence. The real secret is timing. In speaking, timing means the unrestrained and simultaneous expression of your feelings and convictions through the medium of self-expression—your appearance, your actions, your words, and your voice. When you say the same thing, at the same time, with your facial expression, gestures, words, and voice, your timing is right and you develop maximum power.

There are two indispensables in the development of good timing. First, you must thoroughly understand and firmly believe in the idea you are advancing. Second, you must give unrestrained expression to your feelings.

Suppose you had something of substantial importance to tell to a friend of yours. Once you have entered your friend's home and the usual pleasantries are exchanged, you then sit down to have a chat. Finally, in a singsong voice and while focusing on a new picture on the wall you say, "By the way, there is something important I ought to tell you about." Now, compare that with your entering in a rather businesslike fashion, disposing of the greetings very quickly, and before being seated, saying, "John, I have something very important to tell you." And you say this with a serious expression on your face, while you look him in the eye and point to him on the word *you*. Your appearance, action, words, and voice all said the same thing at the same time. You communicated quickly and with impact.

There are so many things you can communicate with proper timing, so that the listener's mind is with you, over and beyond the thoughts you have expressed in words. Certain people in the public eye are masters at this, which may explain their success. Joan Rivers is one of them. She can tell a story in semilaughter with relaxed hand gestures, and her timing is always flawless. She pokes fun at herself, her childhood, her home life—extracting humor out of chaos—getting laughs, not pity. All this because she communicates so well and comes across so genuinely. Even her extreme exaggerations are accepted with glee.

One of the greatest radio comedians of all time, Jack Benny, was able to make the switch to TV because he used body language as effectively as voice language. Invariably someone on his television show made a cutting remark about his image of being a miser. He was always shocked. His reaction was to shout a *"Well!!!"* or a *"Cut that out!"* as he folded his arms and turned his head to the left. The camera caught a close-up of his pained facial expression and the entire house roared with laughter. The timing was flawless. The result, completely predictable.

Comedienne Phyllis Diller displays her timing of professional caliber in another way. Early in her career she developed a very contagious laugh. She attaches it directly to the last word of a punch line. Before the audience has started chuckling, her own laugh has greatly influenced the crowd, and roaring laughter follows. She never misses. Her sense of timing defies description. On occasion she will have a secondary punch line to unfold the innuendo with which she has already produced a laugh. Before she speaks it, she gives the audience that naughty look and a small piece of her infectious laugh and the entire audience is laughing even before they hear her follow-up punch line. She completely controls the reaction of her audience through expert timing.

You don't have to be a star performer to capitalize on good timing. It's something one can use to utmost advantage on a daily basis. The whole idea is to be completely aware of its importance and its implementation. Ask yourself, when a conversation has gone wrong, "Was my timing off?" In many instances you'll discover that better timing would have produced better results.

One last word about timing. It comes naturally only when you have become totally sensitized to it. Until then, it requires your sincere attention by practicing. That's right. We're back to the mirror and the tape recorder. Practice your timing while watching yourself as you talk, convincingly, to the person in the glass. And remember the exercise of taping yourself while you're on the phone? Well, that wouldn't help you here, because only your side of the conversation gets on tape. However, there are many instances these days when a tape recorder is placed at the center of the table around which a business meeting is held. (This releases a secretary from having to take notes, and the whole content of the meeting is later transcribed, with copies distributed.) Well, if you are in commmand of the situation, why not listen to the tape soon after the meeting to evaluate your timing—and that of the others—for self-training through observation. Even if the tape is not in your complete jurisdiction, you can always ask for it—to check on a few details—and get a lesson on timing out of it.

So, practice, and that way become acutely aware of your timing. It will be a tremendous asset.

8
Look For
a Public Platform
Regularly

No question about it, being a good communicator requires good speaking ability. If you want to sell anyone any idea or a product, you have to be able to convince your audience that what you are selling is essential and outstanding. But after you've mastered the techniques that work well in day-to-day, one-to-one meetings and presentations, how do you move up to those that really cause tension and jitters—speaking before groups of people? The answer is that you can start small, but you do have to *start*. You must do something about it on a regular basis. It's like exercising a muscle—the more you do, the stronger it gets.

At first, your public speaking can easily take place at staff meetings, sales conferences, departmental get-togethers, or the gathering of any small group with which you are involved. If you are to give a talk to a group, regardless of size, you immediately begin to think about what you are going to say and exactly how you are going to say it. And going through the whole ordeal does two things for you. First, it makes you think about the right words to use. Second, it gives you the experience of communicating with many people all at the same time.

Speaking to many people is much like the baseball player who, just before his turn at the plate, will swing two or three bats all at the same time. Then, when his turn comes, he discards all but one of the bats and now the single bat feels so light that he's ready to powder the ball on the very first pitch. It's the same with speaking. If you can do a good job at the podium, it follows that speaking to one or two or three people at a time, and doing it effectively, becomes unusually simple.

Therefore, because of the many benefits to be derived, you should begin to make certain that you create opportunities for yourself to do some public speaking. If you have never done any, there are ways to work up to it gradually. When next you are at a meeting, ask a question. Make it a long one. First use two or three sentences for background purposes and then ask the question. If appropriate, be sure you stand up. It makes a big difference. You may be a little nervous, but you'll find that it isn't as bad as most people think. Now you've given your first speech, short as it

116

may have been. And each time you do this it will become that much easier. Just as soon as you become relatively comfortable at asking long questions, you are ready for the podium. Waste no time. Offer to make a presentation on a subject you are well-grounded in and in which you strongly believe. You can do this with your church group, the Parent/Teachers Association, the service clubs (Lions, Kiwanis, Rotary, for example), or any other organization with which you have contact. If this is not possible, then become a member of the chapter of Toastmasters International nearest you. Actually you should do this anyway. Toastmasters and Toastmistresses chapters are excellent organizations. Their purpose is solely to help individuals become proficient at public speaking. All of the members take turns at making speeches at their meetings. There is a guidebook outlining the various types of speeches, each with an objective, and they have a formal method of evaluation for each speech given. The chapters meet at lunch or dinner. The dues are extremely low but the experience gained is far beyond any monetary value.

THERE AREN'T ENOUGH LEADERS

All through life we keep hearing: "There are many followers but only a few leaders." Know why? The answer is plain and simple. A good leader is invariably also a good public speaker. So it follows that if you want to be a leader, you should concentrate on improving your public-speaking abilities. A leader is one who is good at convincing, who can guide people by stimulating and motivating them. The ability to effectively communicate, therefore, is essential. And good leaders, through their speaking power, can influence their followers far beyond the realms of comprehension. Hitler and Mussolini were prime examples. This is not to say that their motives were always admirable. But the fact remains that when they stood before thousands of people, they exerted a power and influence that defied description.

So much can be learned from a leader. When next you are in a meeting, observe the discussion leader closely. Note how this person guides the conversation of others to bring out the points considered significant. In addition to maintaining control at all times, the discussion leader will also direct pointed questions at the people who have not contributed to draw out their opinions, and always make sure that conclusions are reached prior to adjournment.

Note, too, how the chairperson of a committee or the presiding officer of an association handles a show-of-hands vote. If an affirmative vote is the goal, this type leader will say, "How many vote *yes*?" and, while saying this, will emphatically raise his or her hand. This is followed with, "How many vote *no?*" with the voice lacking enthusiasm and the hand staying down.

There is no question that you can become a leader, if you want to and if you take the necessary action on your part to prepare yourself properly. Point yourself in that direction by looking for a platform. Look for and accept opportunities to make a speech. Then sit down and get organized.

HOW TO ORGANIZE A SPEECH

There are at least two ways in which to compose a speech. Many do it the wrong way. Upon accepting the assignment they immediately start worrying. Then they write the speech, read it, tear it up, and write it again. They start to fret. They engage in extensive research, seeking an idea that will set the audience back on its heels. As the day for the speech approaches, they grow more and more jittery. They get irritable, hard to live with, and finally it develops into a race between a nervous breakdown and the hour of the speech.

That's the hard way. The easy way is to start off by asking yourself a simple question: "What is the most helpful thing that can be done for this audience?" As soon as you arrive at the answer to that question, you have the basis for your talk.

An audience rarely expects you to tell them things that they don't already know. Ordinarily the closer you are to your listeners' thinking, the more they like your speech. People like to see themselves in your speech. They're happy when you confirm their ideas.

When you get your newspaper on the morning after you have attended a ball game, what's the first thing you read? A complete recap of what you saw. Why do you do that? You want to live those moments over again. If there was a controversial occurrence during the game, and the reporter interprets it as you did, don't you like him a little bit more than if his views were opposed to yours? Everybody is like that. People like it when you confirm their ideas.

Organizing your speech is no big deal. Once you have decided what you can do to help your audience, you can begin to assemble your data. Get a memo pad and carry it around with you. Whenever you get an idea about the subject on which you are going to speak, jot it down—one idea per page. Be alert for current ideas and events that you can relate to your subject. Audiences like to have you refer to happenings with which they are familiar. As you write these notes, be sure to indicate the particular feature of your speech to which that idea belongs.

Several days before your speech, take your memo pad, tear out the pages, and separate the ideas by features. If any research is necessary, you can now do it on a specific basis, to offer proof or furnish historical or other facts. Then proceed to lay out your speech.

Number one will be your "conditioner." This may be a complimentary remark for your audience, a quip, a word of appreciation, a funny story having relevance to the title of your talk, or a combination of all four. The purpose of the conditioner is to relax your audience and set the stage for the ideas you are going to advance in your speech.

Number two will be the keynote, or theme, of your talk. This is where you tell those in the audience what you hope to do for them. It may be some benefit they will enjoy or some idea you hope to explore with them.

Number three will be the first feature of your talk. It should be the feature with which your audience is most likely to agree. If you have a controversial feature that you feel you must bring in, leave it for later. It's best that you obtain agreement first.

Number four will be your second, third, and fourth features. Try hard never to have more than four. If you can limit your talk to three features, that's better still. As you bring in each feature, be sure you state the philosophy and also give an illustration. It doesn't matter which you cover first, as long as you include both elements.

Number five is your close. This is your bid for action. It is here that you tell your listeners what you hope they will do about the subject you've been discussing.

By following this simple pattern in laying out your talk, it will keep the subject matter clear in your mind and in well-organized form. Accordingly, it will come across just as clearly and as well-organized to the audience.

To show exactly how this all works, let us assume that I am preparing a speech on the the very subject we have been discussing—how to organize a speech. The outline or layout would look like this.

Title: "Organizing a Speech"
1. CONDITIONER
   Compliment, quip, appreciation, funny story
2. KEYNOTE, OR THEME
   What you hope to do for audience
3. FIRST FEATURE (get agreement from audience)
   Philosophy
   Illustration
4. SECOND FEATURE
   Philosophy
   Illustration
   THIRD FEATURE
   Philosophy
   Illustration
5. CLOSE
   Bid for action

In following the pattern of the preceding outline in preparing a speech, you may have written out the entire talk, word for word. You have most likely rearranged sentences to make them sound clearer, replaced weak words with strong ones, and underlined the words you plan to emphasize. Now you're really prepared. However, don't take the written speech with you. Leave it home or at the office. If you take it along, the tendency is to set it down on the rostrum and proceed to read it. That's the worst thing you can do. Audiences don't like you to read to them. A talk is one thing; a reading session is another. The two don't mix.

I have been to hundreds of luncheons and dinners where the main speaker was a president or vice-president of a large corporation. Here is what usually happens. The master of ceremonies, after the usual welcoming remarks, proceeds to introduce the guest speaker. He does this by *reading* a long, drawn-out biography of the speaker prepared for him by the public relations department at the speaker's company. It contains *everything* the man ever did, including his having been a scoutmaster decades ago. Finally it's the speaker's turn. While the audience applauds, he smiles (the last smile to be seen on his face for the duration) and then utters a few sentences to tell how "delighted" he is "to be here." Reaching for his bifocals, he opens the cover of the three-ring binder containing the speech prepared for him by his public relations department. (It had been placed on the lectern for him even before the meal was served.) And from this point on he buries his nose in the script as he reads it, word for word, in a boring monotone. Every so often he gets fouled up, and you wonder how this can happen while he's reading something typed in all caps and double spaced. The reason is that he's never read it before this moment—"just didn't get a chance." So an unusual word or phrase throws him. After what seems like an eternity you finally hear those welcome words, "In conclusion. . . ." There are still several paragraphs to go, but they are tolerable because at least you know that the end is near. As the monotone slows down and the end is virtually in sight, he adds insult to injury. He says, "Incidentally, ladies and gentlemen, if you would like a copy of my remarks here today, you will find mimeographed copies by the door on your way out." Just think, I could have been spared all this agony and read his talk at my leisure and then only the points that were of interest to me.

He closes by making one final mistake. He says, "Thank you very much for listening." It's true that the audience deserves thanks for having suffered through it all. But it is wrong for a public speaker to end his presentation with a thank you. If he did a good job and had a good message, the audience should be thanking him. So adopt this rule right now: When you speak to a group and you've completed your close, your bid for action, you don't end up by saying thank you in any form whatsoever. Know that you did something for that audience. Hold your head up high. If you're stuck for a last sentence, say something like "You were a fine audience" or "I enjoyed being with you." Anything except thank you.

And to avoid giving boring speeches like the one just described, *use only outline notes* on cards—just enough to keep your talk in proper sequence. The rest will take care of itself. You will probably end up changing the wording here and there. Or you will not use the fine grammar that you had worked so hard to achieve. But all that doesn't matter. You will have used your own natural words and it will have all come from the heart. When you are communicating with an audience straight from your heart, it shows. Any grammatical errors you make will go unnoticed. They *feel* what you are saying. They're not looking to pick your English apart.

Do it this way for ten or twelve times and I guarantee you that by then you will have enough courage to *leave the notes in your pocket.* And when you do, you will give the best speech of your life. And every speech after that will be progressively better. You will have become a leader to whom speaking before a group is no longer a chore but a delightful experience. And after each successful talk, you feel even better than the time before.

During a recent interview Bob Hope was asked if he would ever retire. He said, "I've thought about it—but I don't think so. You feel so good after each performance. It's like getting an injection of new life. I doubt that I will ever give *that* up."

Get on a platform and get an injection.

9
Gain the
Upper Hand

An article in *Reader's Digest* magazine, based on a survey, contained the following:

> Americans are very sloppy talkers. They slur and mumble and fail to get their message across. Only 5 out of every 100 have a pleasant and effective speaking voice. Anyone can cultivate this. Many companies—Westinghouse, Allied Chemical, American Cyanamid amongst them—have hired speech specialists to train their salespeople and executives. When, through recordings, they were able to hear their own voices, 9 out of 10 claimed they sounded monotonous. Most people have speaking voices that are much too high.

When they are able to hear their own voices as other people do, most are displeased and then strive to produce a lowering of the voice.

Try whispering. It is an excellent remedy for lazy tongues and stiff upper lips since this forces you to enunciate clearly. By whispering you get the feel of lip, tongue, and jaw movements. To improve and sound mellow like a cello, move the lips more, open the mouth wider, and look in the mirror when you are practicing. Go slow on *y*s, hold *w*s, keep the sound of *l* and *r*. Keep it slow and low. A fast talker is always suspect, hard to follow even if honest.

As you can see from the above, many of the things we have already said in this book come up repeatedly. Much has been written about how poorly Americans speak and the subject is discussed regularly. Yet, so little is done by most individuals to improve themselves in this area. If only people would realize the advantage they would have over others by simply training themselves to speak better, they would take immediate action.

When conducting sales seminars, I spend substantial time on the development of one's personality. A large part of that session is devoted to speaking and the use of diaphragmatic breathing. I record everyone's voice, then teach them how to breathe diaphragmatically, and then record their voices again. When they hear themselves in both the before and after tapes, they are stunned. So am I at noting how few had ever heard their recorded voices before this and how little attention they had ever given to how they speak. And, mind you, these are people who earn their livelihood by practicing the art of convincing through the power of speech.

The assertion "Either you are a born speaker or you are not" is downright foolishness. History has clearly shown that some of our greatest orators were not born with the talent but rather developed it. Obviously, they realized its importance. Demosthenes, for example, was born with a weak voice. He lisped, enunciated poorly, and couldn't pronounce the letter *r*. Yet determination helped him overcome these handicaps. He practiced with pebbles in his mouth, shouted over the roaring breakers on the shores of Phaleron, recited while running uphill, striving to deliver more and more lines with one breath, and rehearsed before a mirror to improve his gestures.

In spite of all these efforts he failed a number of times to win over his listeners. They laughed at him and he was crushed, but not so crushed that he gave up the whole idea. In fact, he actually built an underground chamber where he could project his voice and perfect his delivery without interruption. And for three months at a time he would shave one half of his entire head so that he would resist the temptation to desert his training program and mingle with his friends in "pleasurable pursuits." He overcame all obstacles and became one of the world's greatest orators. Would that more of us could bring ourselves to realize how important it is to speak well. If we gave the matter one-tenth the attention given it by Demosthenes, imagine the improvement that would come about.

We must realize that schools and colleges only take us part of the way. They teach English and all that goes with it. But speaking the language well doesn't get top billing by any stretch of the imagination. It is assumed that one has learned to speak in the early, formative years well enough to get along. It is also assumed that the schooling we receive will round off the edges. These are definite fallacies. The truth is that little or no importance is given to the subject, and the teachers, most of whom speak poorly, are a poor influence on the students they teach.

The desire to speak well must be generated through self-motivation. From his early youth Abraham Lincoln took pains to master the powers of language. In *How to Talk*, John Clapp and Edwin Kane go so far as to say that Lincoln owed his political eminence to his "unremitting effort to use his mother tongue skilfully and persuasively." There is at least one remark of his own on the matter that has been carefully recorded. After the Cooper Union Address in 1860, Lincoln left New York in company with an elderly acquaintance who asked him this question: "I want very much to know how you got this unusual power of 'putting things.' It must have been a matter of education. No man has it by nature alone. What has your education been?" Lincoln answered:

> Well, as to education, the newspapers are correct. I never went to school more than six months of my life. But, as you say, this must be a product of culture in some form. I have been putting the question you ask me to myself while you have been talking. I say this: that among my earliest recollections, I remember how when a mere child, I used to get irritated when anybody talked to me in a way I could not understand. I don't think I ever got angry at anything else in my life. But that always disturbed my temper and has ever since. I can remember going to my little bedroom, after hearing the neighbors talk of an evening, with my father, and spending no small part of the night walking up and down and trying to make out the exact meaning of some of their, to me, dark sayings. I could not sleep, though I often tried to, when I got in such a hunt after an idea, until I caught it; and when I thought I had got it, I was still not satisfied until I had repeated it over and over, until I had put it in language plain enough, as I thought, for any boy I knew to comprehend. This was a kind of pas-

sion with me, and it has stuck by me; for I am never easy now, when I am handling a thought, till I have bounded it north and bounded it south, and bounded it east and bounded it west. Perhaps that accounts for the characteristics you observe in my speeches, though I never put the two things together before.

The poor country boy in his lonely frontier room had already addressed himself to the essential problem in effective communication of thought. The power he began to develop, growing with the years, was to carry him far ahead of the multitude whose early advantages were so much greater than his but who had not learned to adapt their thoughts to the persons they addressed.

THE POWER OF THE SPOKEN WORD

We are all striving for success in life. It may be in varying degrees, for what is considered success by some is failure to others, but on a daily basis we spend much time and effort trying to achieve the measure of success we have as a goal. The formula for success is very hard to define. Ask successful people what their personal formula was and they'll usually tell you that they either worked hard or were very lucky. Many will say, "I happened to be in the right place at the right time." But whatever the case, if you dig deep enough, you will find that there *is* one common denominator. Amazingly enough it's rarely mentioned. It is simply this: Almost everything we do and most of the success we attain depends to a tremendous extent on our *ability to convince others.* And this convincing process, which may take the form of advertising, public relations, image building, meetings, conventions, telephone calls, is as complex as the human brain. Yet one thing is certain. One of the most effective ways to convince anyone of anything always has been, and always will be, in personal face-to-face communication. And at that point it is narrowed down to our ability to speak well enough to convince. The better speaker always wins.

We really don't stop to consider just how powerful the spoken word really is. In fact, we tend to joke about it. Expressions like "Joe has the gift of gab" or "Mary can talk her way out of anything" are often accompanied with a smile or chuckle. The fact remains, however, that people who are clever convincers are also good speakers. They get their points across clearly, dramatically, and with impact. They have tremendous power.

This power, though, is underestimated by a majority of the people. Many think that the written word is just as effective. Never will a letter do the same convincing job that you can do in person. Certain dimensions are missing: you, your facial expressions, the warmth of your personality, and most importantly the way you speak.

Advertising executives will argue that television does the best convincing job in the world. They produce sales figures to show movement of products. By promoting to the masses through television, they claim, they can get Mr. and Mrs. America to go to the supermarket or self-service chain store and select a particular product from the shelf—only because they saw it advertised on television and the brand name was permanently embedded in their subconscious minds.

This may all be true. But they forgot one very important aspect of the whole theory. If the product had not been displayed on a shelf, it could not have been selected for purchase by the consumer. And how did it get on that shelf? Not automatically and not through sheer magic. It got there because a salesperson called on a decision maker for the store or chain of stores. Face to face and through verbal expertise this salesperson *convinced* somebody to designate X number of feet of shelf space for the product and did so by proving just how much promotion, on TV and otherwise, the product had gotten and would continue to get. And even after all this has been accomplished, the salesperson continues to make periodic, routine calls to make sure that the amount of shelf space that was assigned is still there. If it has shrunk any, the proper person has to be convinced all over again. And all of this has to be done face to face—through the power of the spoken word. That's how it all happens and the process will never change.

How amusing it is when you hear certain space-age forecasters contend that the day is not far away when the salesperson will be extinct. Everything, they claim, will be done with computers, videophones, telex. How ridiculous. Our economy is based on goods and servcies sold daily, face to face, through the spoken word. To change that would be disastrous. Just imagine what would happen to our economy if the over ten million salespeople in the United States stayed home for one week without *speaking* to a single prospect or customer. The thought alone is frightening.

You might ask, "Well, why focus so much on selling?" Because all of us sell. We sell ourselves and our ideas constantly, and we do it by speaking to someone or to a group of people. We sell our way into a new job or a raise or a promotion.

Have you noticed how little direct mail you get these days from candidates running for public office? They put most of their money in television. They want to convince people by *talking* to them—even if it is through a picture tube. They know that the impact is so much greater than a written communication. The famous TV debates between John F. Kennedy and Richard Nixon certainly proved that. Until the debates were held, JFK's chances were considered only fair; but we all know what happened. Since then politicians have been fighting like panthers to get TV exposure. Debates, rallies, anything that allows them to talk to the people.

Yes, the spoken word is, without question, one of the most powerful tools we own. How could we possibly not strive to use it wisely and effectively?

IT'S A NEVER-ENDING PROCESS

Like any other area of self-improvement, impressive speaking requires constant attention. It isn't a subject one can study, absorb, acquire the skills it affords, and then relax, knowing that the job is completed. It needs regular review with periodic appraisals of one's delivery and general speaking abilities. But all this is far from boring. Once enough interest in the subject has been generated it becomes exciting and loads of fun—as well as rewarding. The stimulation and satisfaction derived from making a good speech or doing a good convincing job on another person or group of persons cannot be described. You come away with a wonderful feeling of euphoria, a new lease on life, a glow. You know you did it well and you enjoyed it. And like the stonemason who builds a cathedral and then takes pride in his work each time he passes by, you can recall the things you said and how you said them and enjoy again the excitement inwardly produced.

After repeated experiences of this type you reach the point where preparing what you plan to say becomes exciting. You get a charge just thinking about it. Imagine how much fun Billy Mathews must have had when he prepared himself for possible questions from his constituents. He was a congressman from Florida back in the days of prohibition. At a large meeting he was asked a question for which he was fully prepared. He had even rehearsed the answer to ensure proper inflection at the right places. This was his answer:

> I had not intended to discuss this controversial subject at this particular time. However, I want you to know that I do not shun a controversy. On the contrary. I will take a stand on any issue at any time regardless of how fraught with controversy it may be.
>
> You have asked me how I feel about whiskey.
>
> Here is how I stand on this question: If when you say whiskey, you mean the devil's brew, the poison scourge, the bloody monster that defies innocence, dethrones reason, destroys the home, creates misery and poverty, yea literally takes the bread from the mouths of little children; if you mean the evil drink that topples the Christian man and woman from the pinnacles of righteous, gracious living into the bot-

tomless pit of degradation and despair, shame, helplessness and hopelessness, then certainly I'm against it with all of my power.

But, if, when you say whiskey, you mean the oil of conversation, that philosophic wine, the ale that is consumed when good fellows get together, that puts a song in their hearts and laughter on their lips and the warm glow of contentment in their eyes. If you mean Christmas cheer. If you mean the stimulating drink that puts the spring in the old gentleman's step on a frosty morning. If you mean the drink that enables a man to magnify his joy and his happiness and to forget, if only for a little while, life's great tragedies and heartbreaks and sorrows. If you mean that drink the sale of which pours into our treasuries untold millions of dollars, which are used to provide tender care for little crippled children, our blind, our deaf, our dumb, our pitiful aged and infirm, to build highways and hospitals, and schools, then certainly I am in favor of it.

This is my stand and I will not compromise.

I'm sure he smiled widely at the end of his answer. I'm also sure his audience loved every word. As for Billy Mathews, the glow must have been obvious.

I assume that you are substantially interested in

talking your way to success—or you wouldn't have read this far. For this you are to be complimented. But this book should be only the beginning in the process of improving your speaking abilities. Research the subject thoroughly. Read as much as you can find in any library or bookstore. And, of course, listen more carefully when others speak, to appreciate the good and note the bad. By keeping constantly aware of the many facets of this subject you will automatically tend to improve yourself.

Obviously, everything there is to be known about impressive speaking is not in this book. The poor habits of speaking are many and varied. The corrective measures are equally numerous. I don't think anyone will ever put them all down on paper and feel that nothing has been left out. But at least you can reason that these pages have taken you deeper into a subject which is of concern to you. And if you have picked up only a few ideas that will help you, it will have all been worthwhile.

There is a standing joke about the successful business executive who makes use of every minute of his time and who never settles for mediocrity in anything. When he's traveling, he never lets up. As soon as he unpacks his bag in a hotel room, he reaches for the Gideon bible and begins to pencil in the corrections.

While this book is certainly not a bible, you are still cordially invited to pencil in the corrections during each successive reading. In so doing, you will be giving much more thought to the ways through which you *will* become a more impressive speaker, a better convincer and much more successful in business and in life. Most worthwhile, isn't it?